CW01674247

Data Literacy for the Workplace

Michael D. Lairson

Copyright © 2022 Michal D. Lairson

All rights reserved.

ISBN: 9798405521534

DEDICATION

This book is dedicated to all of those who have worked by my side to make data available and to implement data-drive decision making in our workplaces.

DATA LITERACY FOR THE WORKPLACE

CONTENTS

Acknowledgments i

Introduction 1

What is Data Literacy? 3

1 Data 5

2 Literacy 9

3 Role of Data in the Workplace 11

It Starts with good Data 15

4 Gathering and Organizing Data 17

5 Identifying Types of Data 25

6 Judging the Quality of Data 31

7 Detecting Bias 35

Reading to Understand 43

8 Types of Analytics 45

9 Methods for Examining Data 51

10 Introduction to Descriptive Statistics 57

11 Data Visualized 63

Presenting to Convey Meaning 73

12 Begin with a Question 75

13 Select your Data 79

14 Analyze your Data 83

15 Present your Data 91

Making Data Driven Decisions 97

16 Use Data to Inform your Decisions 99

17 Validate, Adjust and Improve Your Decisions 103

18 Artificial Intelligence and Machine Learning 105

Appendices

A Glossary of Terms 107

B Abecedarian Lucubration 113

C MySQL Data Types 115

D SQL Database Data Types 117

E Oracle/PSQL Data Types 119

F MS Access Data Types 121

DATA LITERACY FOR THE WORKPLACE

ACKNOWLEDGMENTS

I began work on this book in my head years ago. For that I would acknowledge everyone for whom I have ever built an analysis or visualization. Data literacy is required to effectively analyze and visualize data, but it is also extremely helpful when the recipients of those analyses can effectively understand and use those analyses. I finally decided to begin writing in November 2021 and did so in relative secrecy. No one other than my family knew why I was spending hours in my home office after my workday had ended. I would like to thank my wife Susan, and my boys Robert and David for supporting me and allowing me to steal time to write. I appreciate that what I have is rare in that I get to do work that I love each day and then spend time doing what I love after work and all the while feel surrounded by love. My worst day is often better than other's best day, and for that I thank God.

INTRODUCTION

I have had many jobs in my career. I have been fortunate enough to be able to leverage each phase of my career to pivot a bit for each subsequent phase to eventually land where I sit today. I began my career as a Technical Writer in the early 1990s. I have not always enjoyed writing but fell in love with it in college. Prior to working on my degree in English, I had taken some classes in instructional design while I was a Middle School Education major. I quickly gathered enough data to know that was not the career path I was looking for. I did, however, enjoy the instructional design class and writing instructional material, so technical writing made sense. This also helped me make my first pivot and begin my next career as an Instructional Designer and Performance Consultant. Somehow, I came back to teaching while hanging on to writing. I began to become more interested in the measurement and testing elements of instruction. I began a graduate program of my own design and earned a Master of Education degree in Instructional Systems Technology with an emphasis on Educational Measurement and Statistics. This led me to my next pivot where I began working for a software company on the Software Certification team where I produced the exams that individuals would take to become certified. My favorite part of this job was performing the psychometrics on the test results and the analyses to determine which questions were effective and what the cut score should be for each exam. I also discovered business analytics during this time and spent some time teaching and developing analytics for customers. This is when I wrote my first book and discovered the joy of pulling all the favorite parts of my career together. I was writing, teaching, and analyzing all at once.

From there I went on to work as a consultant implementing software and analytics tools for many different businesses around the world. During that time, I penned a few more small books and learned a lot about how business use data. Not many of them were using the data to make business decisions. I have since come in off the road and settled into a data science position for a great company that is in the business of helping other businesses grow and prosper. I had found the final piece of the puzzle for my career. I write. I teach. I analyze. I help other companies succeed. It is difficult to not at the data I gathered over my career and not come to the decision that I am doing the right job for me.

I have reflected for a long time on why I wanted to write this book, and what my goal for the book would be, and even a bit about what makes me think I have something to share that others would appreciate. Amid that reflection, I realized that I really needed to write this book for me, if for no one else. My personality is one that has me over-thinking and over-analyzing every aspect of everything I do to the point that data and analysis almost literally drives every decision I make. I live for data and they are what help me live. I might even find organizing my thoughts on data here to be somewhat therapeutic as well.

So that's what I get out of the exercise of writing about data literacy, but I want you to get something from this as well. With any luck, it will not feel like exercise. I encounter people daily who I believe would benefit from absorbing some of the topics I discuss here. I firmly believe that if everyone in the workplace, regardless of what type of work that is, had a grasp of data literacy then businesses would succeed and grow much easier and communities would thrive, and people would have many fewer conflicts. After all, making decisions based on the data rather than doing whatever the loudest or most senior or most related to the company owner says you should do would make those meetings afterward much more comfortable.

My goal for this book is to help you along your journey to data literacy. I have purposely kept this book short with small easy to read chapters. I appreciate that most businesspeople do not have a lot of time to commit to reading, especially on a topic that is somewhat complex and intricate. It does not matter where you currently are along that journey, I believe the way I have organized this book you will find something that will help you along your own journey or at least help you understand where others are in their data literacy development in order to better communicate with them. When I sat down to plan this book, I thought about literacy and what it means to be literate, and how one becomes literate. I thought about how people learn a new language. First, we have to want to learn a new language, or come to the realization that we must learn a new language. I determined that I should also start by discussing the "alphabet" or in this case, data. It is important to have a baseline knowledge and understanding of the data that make up the reports and analytics and test results that we may encounter in the workplace. You may even be responsible for communicating and creating some of these things. So, after we understand data a bit, we will discuss how to read those data and interpret those data as we use our data literacy to make data-driven business decisions. Literacy is both reading and writing, so I cover communicating with data in the back half of the book and bring it all back to making data-driven decisions.

I begin the discussion of data literacy in the workplace by establishing some foundation upon which to build. In the "What is Data Literacy?" section we will discuss the three elements that make up the title: data, literacy, and the workplace. With that foundation laid, we move into the "It Starts with Good Data" section. Bad data does no one any favors. To benefit from data, you need good, organized, unbiased data that are of the correct type. Once we know what good data look like, we need to be able to read them. In the "Reading to Understand" section we will look at the way data are analyzed, examined, and visualized. Next, in the "Presenting to Convey Meaning" section we put something into action and move to the transmit side of literacy and communication. We will discuss the importance of knowing what question you mean to answer, selecting the data you will use to answer that question, examining, and presenting that data.

Finally, we will wrap things up my taking all that we have learned and begin "Making Data-Driven Decisions." In this final section you will read about using data to inform your decisions, validating those decisions with data, adjusting and refining to improve decisioning, and will touch on artificial intelligence (AI) and machine learning (ML). I throw in a glossary of terms so this book will hopefully be a resource you can return to when discussing data. What would literacy be without a vocabulary, after all?

I have laid out what this book is intended to be, but I want to take a moment to explain some things you will not get out of this book. This is not a mathematics or statistics textbook. [Pause for a sigh of relief.] While being strong at math is necessary for success as a data scientist, this is not a requirement for data literacy. Likewise, we will touch on a few concepts but not dive deeply into data modeling, database management, specific software packages, data visualization, business management, or AI and ML. There are many other resources that you can turn to in order to learn more about these topics. The common pre-requisite for all these topics is data literacy, and that is what we will begin exploring right now.

WHAT IS DATA LITERACY?

In the field of data science there are many definitions for what a data scientist is or is not. A data scientist who believes one must hold a Ph.D. in statistics to bear the title will surely scoff at the notion that someone who is adept with spreadsheet programs and generating charts is a data scientist. This debate will rage on for some time, but one thing I believe all data scientists will agree upon is the need for everyone, not just the data scientists, to be data literate.

Exactly what makes one data literate can also certainly be a subject for debate. Literacy in general is typically described as being able to read and write well enough to communicate and understand. Data literacy is not much different, except we are not concerning ourselves with using the correct word tense or knowing the difference between "your" and "you're" in our communications. We are however, quite concerned with receiving and transmitting the meaning within our analyses of data as clearly and accurately as possible.

The concept of data literacy in the workplace further focuses our data communication on topics meaningful within a workplace. While data literacy could help you win the office fantasy football pool, herein we will discuss using data to not only make your job easier and more productive, but to help you and your business to make business decisions that are based in an understanding of the data.

For the purposes of this book, I am using the following definition:

In order to be data literate in the workplace, one must:

- Know which data are appropriate to use for answering a particular business question.
- Have the ability to read charts and graphs in order to interpret the data.
- Understand the path of data from its source to the data visualization.
- Know how to represent data based on the type of analysis you are performing.
- Recognize improperly used data, biased analyses, and misleading data representations.
- Have the ability to communicate about data with others who may not be as data literate.

1
DATA

Data are everywhere. If that statement sounds strange to you because I use "are" rather than "is" then perhaps that gives us the first thing to learn about data. Technically "data" is the plural form of "datum" meaning that data are more than one datum. Common vernacular has made is perfectly acceptable to use "data" in the singular form as well as the plural form when describing data. I very rarely have a need to use the singular "datum." I occasionally catch myself referring to data in the singular as well. I prefer when I and others use plural when discussing data. It is one way I can tell right away that someone I am speaking with may be data literate. This is not a reliable way to determine one's data literacy, but it may very well be a leading indicator.

Data are everywhere, and in everything you will find data and are able to describe everything using data. Every innovation seems to take advantage of data more and more. Technology is improving. Data processing is becoming faster. Data storage is becoming cheaper. And now that cloud technology is prevalent, there are more ways to access and share data than ever. Data are the commodity of the future. Technologies will come and go. Businesses will open and close. Inventions will be made. And most certain among these future realities is that data are here to stay and will play a critical role in everything we do.

We describe our past using data. We measure our present using data. And now we predict our future using data. We all use and rely on data constantly. I would argue that in many ways the data are not new. We have always since the development of language used data to describe how things look, feel, and smell. Things have always had dimensions, volumes, and weights. People have always made observations, had opinions, and felt emotions. What is newer and still developing rapidly is how we collect, store, and use data. Companies know more about you than you want them to. Nearly every online interaction you have generates data that businesses use to market their products, sell their products, develop new products, and service those products. Thousands of terabytes of data are collected every day, and keeping pace is the ability to store and access those data. We also have spies plugged in among us in our homes. It seems like all of our electronic devices are listening and remembering things. These devices communicate with other devices and companies that collect these data. They make our lives more convenient, but the price of that convenience is data that companies can use to sell you more conveniences. While the internet of things (IOT) devices are relatively new, the collection of data from consumers is not new. If you have a frequent shopper card or store credit card you are providing data with every trip to the store. I have heard stories of stores predicting pregnancy and sending coupons to pregnant women before they knew themselves that they were pregnant. I cannot verify the accuracy of that story, but I can verify that data and statistical analyses can and does provide such predictions to companies examining our shopping patterns and history.

So what does this data look like? One trip to the grocery store generates more data than I can describe here, but consider that your phone in your pocket likely captures information about when and where you are located. The video cameras in the store capture your image entering and moving through the store. The shopper card captures the amount you are spending, the brands you are purchasing, how many of each item and the types of items you purchase. The credit card you use adds to your spending history. Your car likely collects some data as well. Your smart watch knows how many steps you took and what your heart rate was when you passed by the ice cream aisle. All of these data are collected and maybe only a fraction of it is used today to describe you specifically, but much more is used to develop a profile of the shoppers like you. Repositories of big data (unstructured collections of everything that can be collected) and specific databases owned by the companies tracking your data are updated constantly with anything and everything.

If you were to examine this data carefully, you would find that the data can be grouped into two high-level types. Quantitative data are those that are a numerical value of some sort. If the datum is reflecting a value of some kind (amounts, sizes, quantities, counts), then it is quantitative. Quantitative data can be at an interval or ratio level of measurement. The interval level of measurement provides for a defined numerical scale with a particular named, ordered, and known consistent difference between points on the scale. The ratio level of measurement provides for accommodation of absolute zero. A survey question for example that asks you to rate your job satisfaction from 1 to 5 is an interval measurement because there is an order and consistent difference between values. A survey question that asks for your annual income is a ratio level of measurement because there is an order, consistent difference between values, and allows for a zero answer.

Dates and times, in my mind, are somewhere in between quantitative and qualitative, but technically they would be considered quantitative because there are mathematical properties to dates and times since they can be plotted on an axis and it is possible to define one date as being greater than or less than another. Dates are at the interval level of measurement as there is a defined order and consistent difference between values, but there is not concept of a zero value for a date. Times are at the ratio level or measurement as it is possible for zero on the time scale.

It may be obvious that metrics like number of customers, sales revenue totals, product inventories, service case counts, and cost of materials are all examples of quantitative data. Generally speaking, there is a very good chance that any numerical information is what we call quantitative data. Quantitative data can answer questions like "how much?", "how many?", "how often?", and "how long?" using numeric values. Mathematic operations describe these data by totaling, averaging, and using other standard algorithms.

Unless you are involved in some higher technologies that generate data through computer analysis, such as devices that convert images or celestial observations into numeric values without human intervention, you will deal primarily with four modes of quantitative data. Quantity data – counts of things like the number of leads generated during a campaign or the number of individuals who called the help line – is what I consider the base mode of quantitative data. Nearly anything can be counted. More on this when we get to qualitative data. The next mode would be measurements. Physical objects have dimensions, mass, weights, volume, etc. These measurements are reflected numerically on a scale. Our third mode requires some additional mathematical or statistical treatments. This is projected data. Anticipating the amount of revenue to expect from future sales for instance, requires the use of known quantitative data to determine a projected value of that same data in the future. Finally, the last mode is similar to the first. Quantifying qualitative data is not exactly the same as counting physical things but is the assignment of a numerical value to conceptual concepts. You will find this type of data in survey results or reviews on a web site. Often a Likert scale of some type is used to associate opinions with a number in order to calculate an overall average or score. This is not always obvious to the person completing the survey, but behind the scenes, you can be sure that responses like "somewhat agree" are assigned a numerical value for analysis.

The other primary sort of data is qualitative data. These data are sometimes referred to as descriptive data or categorical data and exist primarily at the nominal and ordinal levels of measurement. These data are typically not numerical, but still descriptive of some object or conceptual idea. Qualitative data stored in a database or table are often referred to as attributes or dimensions. Some examples of these data include sales stage, service plan, industry, type, location, and record owner. This list can quite literally go on forever. Recall

I said data are everywhere and everything is data. Anything that provides you some information, no matter how trivial, is data. Qualitative data are also observations that can be assessed and categorized. Qualitative data may come from focus groups, surveys, and interviews. This type of data is not what you may expect to work with when performing an analysis, but qualitative data is very helpful in determining how frequently a characteristic or trait appears in your data. Grouping data by these characteristics are useful in determining parameters for your testing and analysis. If you are doing some sort of research, these qualitative data will help you define your study group. If you are documenting feelings and opinions of customers, employees, or members of the public, this is qualitative data. Performing a statistical analysis of this type of data requires that you morph those data to something quantitative so that you can apply a mathematical treatment.

A useful characteristic of qualitative data is that these data can often be treated as quantitative data. By grouping and counting, you are essentially creating quantitative data using your qualitative data. You will also find that you are using the qualitative data to define categories for which you calculate a value in your analysis. How many sales opportunities are in the closing stage? This type of question is answered with a quantitative value but relies on a grouping by qualitative data. You may also generate quantitative data by performing some calculation using multiple datapoints. For example, calculating the number of hours between a service case's open date and close date, you have a new bit of data that numerically describes the time to resolution for a case. The assignment of a numerical value to qualitative values is another method of using qualitative data in data analysis. A response on a survey, as mentioned earlier, results in quantitative values from qualitative data by assigning a value to an opinion. A Likert scale is standard for most surveys. Consider a survey that asks if you are extremely satisfied, somewhat satisfied, neutral, somewhat dissatisfied, or extremely dissatisfied about some service or product. What you are really providing for study is a rating of -1, -0.5, 0, 0.5, or 1. This quantifiable data can now be used to calculate descriptive statistics that will tell you something about the opinion of a group.

The below diagram further describes characteristics of different types of data. As you continue reading, you will learn specifics about how data are described and defined and how each type of data is used in making data-driven decisions.

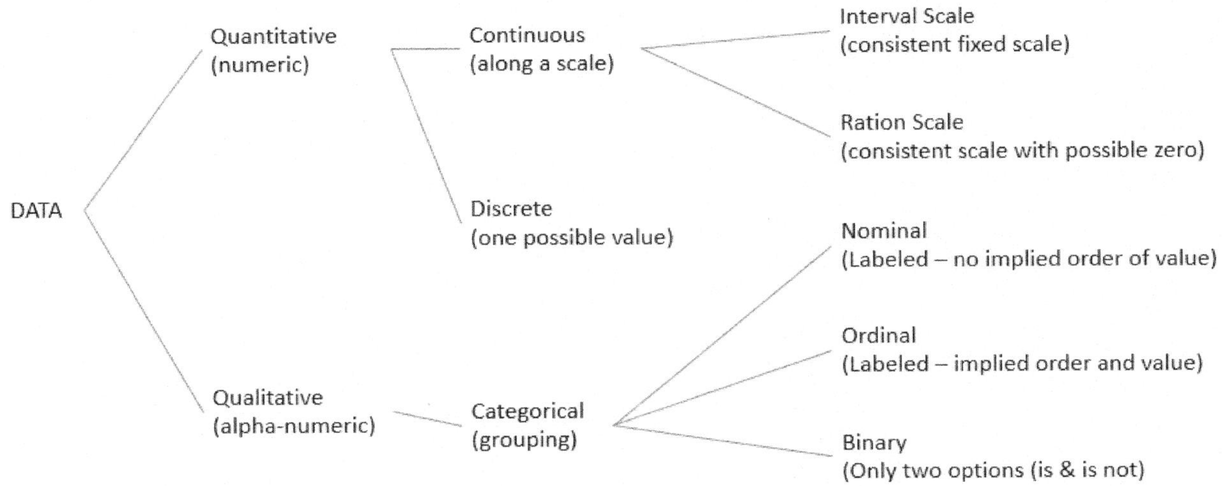

I would like to add a special note here about something that I wish I didn't have to explain to people in the workplace repeatedly. It may seem like a simple concept, but it is apparently difficult for some people to grasp the difference between live data and static data and how to know which they are looking at. Live data is data that is in a database or system that is changing constantly, or at least regularly. These are transactional data, data from systems that are being used for data input. When we look at reports and dashboards presented on the computer, those are typically querying live data to show the current state of those data in the database. The moment those data are displayed on the screen, they could be changing behind the scenes, and you will only see the newest and latest updated data when you refresh or run the report again. It may be obvious, but I will also emphasize that the moment you print or export that report with those data, you are creating a static copy of the data in a file that is no longer being updated. If you were to compare the report you printed yesterday to the same report on the system today, they would likely no longer match.

There exist some datasets that are always static. Data warehouses often contain snapshots of data stored and not overwritten by new data. These data are used to compare data over time and are very useful when wanting to view history of data that normally resides in a transactional system. We cannot rely on live data for historical reporting because the historical data are updated and overwritten. If you were to compare a report of last month's activity in a transactional database and compare it to the historical report from the snapshot data in a data warehouse, they are very likely to not match. I am often surprised by individuals who do this and raise an alarm or form a distrust of the data because they do not understand the difference in live and static data.

2
LITERACY

With the continued emergence of business analytics and data policies and strategies, the need to be data-literate has become a requirement for success. Employees must possess the ability to examine and understand data, share information derived from data, and make sound decisions based on an analysis of data more than ever. As data becomes more accessible to everyone, businesses are looking for ways to leverage their data to improve the business. The only way to effectively do this is to have a data-literate staff. This is a industry-agnostic truth. The need for data literacy crosses all industries and all levels of the company.

Let's begin by understanding what it means to be literate. Literacy is a uniquely human experience that probably began some time during the Bronze Age with hieroglyphics. Symbols or drawings were used to communicate some meaning from the writer to the reader, and the classifications of literate and non-literate were born. If these symbols were being used to describe things, qualitative data was born as well. The Egyptians around this same time began using symbols to represent numbers too. The number 1 was simply a line. Not much has changed there. The number ten was represented symbolically as a bit of rope. One hundred was a coil of rope. We can see there is meaning here. A line is one. Several lines twisted together into a rope is ten, and a coil of this rope is one hundred. These were measures - quantitative data! The Egyptians also had larger numbers too. One thousand is a flower. Ten thousand is a finger. One hundred thousand is a frog. One million is a person on their knees with arms outstretched toward the sky.

It's hard to say when actual analysis of data really began. One could argue that the Egyptians must have been doing some calculating to construct their pyramids. Others may argue that serious analysis probably did not exist until the Pythagoreans started talking math. Either way, data has been around for a long time, and becoming data literate is long overdue.

If literacy is the ability to read to understand, and write to convey meaning, using a common language, can we consider ourselves data literate if we can read and write using numbers and other visuals to convey meaning? Well, yes and no. I think if you can read and write using letters and numbers, you are certainly literate. However, I believe to be data literate you must understand the language of letters and numbers making up your data. Understanding and conveying meaning requires a deeper understanding of the language as well as how we derive meaning using that language of data. We have begun to understand the language a bit in the previous chapter. But to truly understand it well enough to be considered data literate requires a bit more context.

Modern literacy goes well beyond just being able to read and write. In the English language, there are many words that can have many different meanings depending on how and where it is used. In everyday conversation, the intonation of the word can significantly change a word's meaning. Similarly, how data is presented in a visualization can significantly change the message being conveyed by the data. The amount of data you include or exclude can change the message. Data selection, filtering, formatting, aggregations, and where and how it is shared can all affect the meaning that readers take from the data. This means that you will read a presentation of data as well as present your own data based on your level of data literacy.

Your vocabulary also has a lot to do with how well you can read and write in any particular language. Some have an extensive personal lexicon of sesquipedalian locutions. Having a conversation or reading something written by such a person may not mean much to you if you do not share the same vocabulary. You probably do not want to challenge these people to word games either. Just like with any form of communication, in any language, you are not going to effectively communicate if you do not understand their language or they do not understand yours.

There is also an element of storytelling that is very important in data literacy. If you are tasked with explaining something with data, then you must be able to tell a story with those data much like an author paints a picture with words or a teacher designs a lesson plan that builds up to learning something new. Storytelling with data is a discipline all of its own and requires not just the ability to recognize and read data, but to understand it at a level deep enough to share it with others by guiding them on a journey through the data. Most times this storytelling will begin with the most general concepts and navigate deeper into the more complex. This is similar to how teachers will begin with a high-level overview before diving into the particulars of a subject. If you jump directly to the details, you risk losing your audience and failing to deliver your intended message.

I will share a personal story here that I think illustrates the nature of literacy perfectly. When I was in school working on my English degree, I took a creative writing course. One portion of this class was on interpreting the meaning of poems. I love poetry, but I am not a huge fan of trying to interpret some sort of hidden message that the author was not necessarily trying to convey. During this class, one of my classmates interpreted a very popular beautiful poem as some sort of message about the fall of the German empire. I did not agree. The class was then given an assignment to write a poem anonymously and after handing them in, the professor would redistribute them so everyone had someone else's poem to interpret. I was the type of student that liked to make a point through some light rebellion, so I wrote a poem titled Abecedarian Lucubration. The poem consists of one word for every letter of the alphabet, and each of those words is long, difficult to pronounce, obscure, or a combination of these. The poem quite literally described itself with each line. I was very happy when the "German empire guy" received my poem. He gave up pretty quickly, so I shared my poem along with a translation to English that everyone could understand. I later attempted to get the poem published, but was told that my poem was too difficult for the publisher's readership. I will include the poem and translation in the Appendices so it can finally be published thirty years late. There's that rebellion again.

From this example, we can see a few principles applicable to data literacy. If we are unable to understand the language of the message, we will not receive the right message. If we are unable to use the language properly, we will not communicate the right message. If we do not consider the context or provide the necessary context, the message will be lost in translation. The remainder of this book will provide a common language and defined context for understanding and transmitting the right message with our data.

3
ROLE OF DATA IN THE WORKPLACE

Data may very well be your businesses' most valuable and important asset. If you are taking full advantage of data in your workplace, then every moment of every day is affected in some way by data. The term "data-driven" has become almost cliché as companies tout that they are making data-driven decisions and enacting data-driven policies and programs. There is no standard for making such a claim, and since data are everywhere, it would be difficult to argue that companies are not using data for making decisions. I would reason that a business is making data-driven decisions only if those decisions are supported by a valid analysis of those data and presented in some way that supports the decision being made. Data may be used to drive every decision a company makes from pricing to supply chain to hiring to pay scale. You make decisions based on data constantly. The route you drive to work is based on data that you have retained in your mind about drive times, traffic levels, number of potholes, or which route includes the most convenient morning coffee. You decide what to order at that coffee place based on data you have about your preferences for taste, temperature, cost, and which pairs best with the scone you are having for breakfast. This continues for the rest of the day. You are able to make these data-driven decisions on-the-fly in your head because you are intimately familiar with the data.

Your workplace is populated with many others making these personal data-driven decisions every moment of the day. That is the role of data in your person. The role of data in your workplace is not much different, except that you cannot rely exclusively on the data that are in your subconscious database or data you have personally collected through experience. Data are also present and prevalent in the workplace, but for everyone to benefit from these data, they must be captured. Data recorded somewhere that others can access is convenient and may be analyzed. When you order coffee, you are asking the data to inform your decision. When you have a business question to answer, you should ask the data to help support the answer to that question. Unfortunately, most businesses are not very good at collecting and organizing their data, so asking the data to answer questions is either not possible or the results are not very reliable. You can ask me how to perform brain surgery, and I could give you an answer based on the limited data I possess, but I sure would not like to be the one on the operating table or the surgeon about to scramble that patient's brain.

Making data-driven decisions without good data is possibly worse than simply guessing. At least with guessing, you do not have a false level of confidence that the insufficient data may give you. So when I am referring to data in the workplace, I am meaning Complete, Consistent, Clean, Convenient, and Controlled data. Let's call these the Five Cs of good data.

Complete: Complete data are data that provide as much information as possible about a subject. Let's say you are using a Customer Relationship Management (CRM) software to record data about your customers. As a busy salesperson you may not feel like you have the time or need to populate every field for which you have an answer. You may tend to only enter what you know you will need and provide a name, email, and phone number. You skip the address fields. You don't bother with the company size or industry or additional contacts. You skip over the fields that you just don't think are all that important for making this sale. These data are not complete. The company cannot rely on an analysis of which industries are buying more of your product because the industry information is incomplete. Completeness of the data is a team effort as well. It is not enough for you, after having read this book perhaps, to begin collecting all of the data on your customers if you are the only one doing so. Some complete records and some incomplete records provide a biased view of the overall data. This brings us to Consistency of the data.

Consistent: Consistent data is not only consistently complete, meaning everyone is doing their part to record data, it is also consistent in the quality of data. Consistency can be enforced in many ways by the systems in which you are recording the data, but since this is not a book about databases, let's define consistency. We can think about consistency of data in multiple ways. Level of detail is one that often trips companies up when there are multiple systems in play or multiple groups collecting the same data in multiple ways. Let's take a single customer as an example case. The sales team may capture this customer's data as a single record. There is one customer name, one industry, one address. This makes the most sense to the sales team. The service team does not use the customer record from the sales team and captures their own data about the customer. They are supporting each location for this customer, so they have multiple records. Each has the same company name, a location, an industry, and a different address. The finance departments also capture their own data rather than using what has already been collected and they have a billing record for the parent company, but no information on the child company or locations that purchased the product. Capturing complete data is great. Capturing it multiple times in multiple places at different levels of detail creates a lot of confusion when attempting to analyze the data.

Another way to think about consistency is in the format of the data. We will discuss specific advantages and disadvantages of data types later in this book, but for now it is important to know that using the same data type for the same data is important to the future analyses of those data. Some simple decisions about how data will be recorded will pay dividends later. Will we capture this bit of data in UPPER CASE or Title Case (also known as Camel Case)? Will we capture the dates in MM/DD/YYYY format or DD/MM/YYYY format? Are we capturing times in the time zone of the person entering the data, or a specific time zone? Which currency are we using? How many decimal places? What language?

Consistency is also important in who is capturing these data and where these data are being stored. It may not be the most efficient if only one person or group is responsible for capturing your data, though that would likely help with consistency. What is important is that there is a set of guidelines or rules of engagement for the capturing and storing of data. Your company may have or be in the process of creating a data strategy to help regulate the capturing of data and the security of those data. You may even have a master data control system in place that identifies which data are the winner if there is conflicting data. If you are really fortunate, your company has a data strategy that provides for data governance of data to ensure that all of your company's data are complete, consistent, clean, convenient, and controlled. Let's next discuss clean data.

Clean: Clean data is data that is complete and consistent but is also free of bad or garbage data. Things like partial phone numbers and emails are no benefit to you. Entering fake information just to satisfy a required input for instance is detrimental, even if it does get you to the next screen. I sometimes wonder how many records John Doe or Bugs Bunny have in databases across all companies. Another thing that our data science teams are constantly clearing out are characters entered in front of names to force the record to the top of the list when sorted. Back when phonebooks were common in every household, you could see how many companies named themselves "A+" something or prefaced their name with "AAA." This made sense because it forced the company to show up near the top of the list above their competitors. This does not make sense in our workplace data repositories. Do not add a "+" or "!" or other character to the field value to make it bend to your sorting preferences. Also, do not add notes to the name field like "[Duplicate]" or "[Do Not Call]" even if you may find this useful personally. These notes may be valid data that should be captured somewhere. If there is no way to indicate something on your data records that you want to capture, discuss it with your system administrators or data science team rather than enter dirty data. It would be impossible for me to list all of the possible ways to mess up the cleanliness of your data, but I want to share one other thing that, as a data scientist, I absolutely loathe. That is the word "other" in a selection field. The word "other" has probably skewed more analyses that any single word in the data. There are a couple of problems with allowing users to select other in a field. The first is that people are inherently lazy and will select other because it is easier than determining the correct value to select. Another is that system administrators, being people, are also inherently lazy and would rather provide "other" as an option than maintain a lookup table of valid values by adding new values as they are discovered. This is exacerbated by the data scientists or others doing some analysis who insist that there must be a value selected in the field. Upon receiving this requirement, the system administrators will make the field required, which generates many complaints from the users. Upon receiving enough complaints, the system administrators will invariably add or make "other" the default value in the field. Now the inherently lazy users do not even need to select anything in this field to move on. We are, after all, creatures of convenience. So let's talk about Convenient data.

Convenient: Capturing good complete, consistent, clean data is pointless if we lock it away and keep anyone from using them. For data to be used effectively, people need to be able to access them and have the tools necessary to query the data. I have seen many instances of overly protective owners of data who do not want to share their data out of fear that it will somehow be corrupted, used improperly, devalued, or taken away. This is really a bit silly, but the reason there is a need for master data governance and a corporate data strategy. There are a number of ways with technology that data can be shared while still protected, so this really should not be an issue. There are also a number of regulations that govern what particular people can and cannot access. Some personal identifiers (PID), a subset of personally identifiable information (PII), like account numbers and Social Security Numbers are protected by law and must be kept secure. You may also be affected by things like the Health Insurance Portability and Accountability Act of 1996 (HIPAA) that control which data are sharable without permission of the data's owner (the person for whom the data is related).

When I say that data should be convenient for others to access, I am not condoning that you need to share all data with others. You may keep a list of things or have some personal research you have done that really has no benefit to others, especially others in the workplace. The data I refer to are the data that are collected on behalf of the company and stored on company systems. Making sales data available to service and marketing data available to sales and so on is only going to be beneficial to the company. Many companies are finding that their data assets are so important and valuable to the company that they are creating Chief Data Officer (CDO) positions in the executive suite to provide some oversight and control of data.

Controlled: Data that are out of control are unorganized and difficult to use. Some levels of control are necessary to have data in the workplace that really work for the company and support data-driven decision making. Your business should have some controls in place to regulate what data are collected, how those data are maintained, where those data are kept, and who can access them. Convenient data may be uncontrolled, but controlled data need not be inconvenient. With the right controls in place, the company's data are made available to all who have a business need for them. With the right controls in place, the company's data is protected from corruption. Controlled data adheres to rules from how the data is collected, cleaned, accessed, and eventually archived. Some data has a shelf-life and just becomes extra noise after a while. You do not want to make data-driven decisions using data that are expired and hold no meaning in the present.

Data controls may also be put in place to move data to a data warehouse through an extract, transform, and load (ETL) process. Your company may find benefit in copying or moving data from active business systems to a centralized data warehouse. This way access to the data can be provided and controlled from a single data repository.

Once your business has data that is complete, consistent, clean, convenient, and controlled you can take full advantage of those data to make data-driven decisions by examining the data. As a data literate individual you will be able to read and understand data, gain value from data visualizations, answer business questions using data, and communicate your findings to others. That is what I intend to help you do with this book.

IT STARTS WITH GOOD DATA

We have touched on what makes data good data. The five Cs is a good start. Of course, our data needs to be Complete, Consistent, Clean, Convenient, and Controlled. This is only part of what makes data good data for analyses and data-driven decision making. In order to make valid decisions with our data, those data need to be valid. Just as there are many ways for data to be what I call garbage data (misspelled, incomplete, extra characters, etc.) there are many ways to render data invalid. To this point we have discussed data at more of a micro level. Specific records and fields on a specific record may be bad or incomplete, and that is definitely a problem. We can also have issues at the macro level when data are gathered improperly and disorganized. Different types of data provide different analytic possibilities. Certain types of data are conducive to different types and levels of analysis and can be used to answer some business questions but shouldn't be used to answer others. Of course, the quality of our data is important, and we have begun discussing this, but it is possible to have pristine data in our databases but have data that is poor quality for use in decision making. We may even find that the same data are able to answer the same question differently dependent on the quality of the data and the bias we introduce as we examine those data.

With the next four chapters, we will discuss how we can properly gather and organize data for our analyses. We will identify many different types of data and how they can be used for our data-driven decisions. We will discuss the quality of data in more detail, at both the record level and the dataset level. Finally, we will look at how we can introduce bias and how to limit the bias of our analyses so that we are making valid decisions with our data.

I often use "Valid" to describe data and analyses. I would say that valid data will adhere to the five Cs but should also follow the V.A.L.I.D. model shared below. More on this model in the chapter on verifying the quality of our data.

Valid data meet the following criteria:

Verifiable. Valid data come from a verifiable credible source.

Avoids Bias. Valid data are collected and analyses using methods that limit bias as much as possible.

Legitimate. Valid data are statistically relevant and can legitimately support claims made using them.

Interpretable. Valid data are meaningful, relatable, and understandable. Ambiguous data are not valid.

Decisional. Valid data lead to data-driven decision making.

4
GATHERING AND ORGANIZING DATA

Data may be collected in a number of ways. You may be entering information into a computer application that stores the data. You may conduct surveys that collect information. You may have computer systems that automatically log activity. You might just keep a notebook of important things you want to remember. Forms, applications, surveys, system logs, focus groups, observations, and tests are just a handful of sources from which you may collect data or use to gather data about a subject.

The collection of data is a prerequisite of any research or study. Gathering and organizing data on specific variables is what will enable you to answer questions and evaluate success in your business. Data are more than just numbers and measures. Qualitative data along with quantitative data are necessary components when making any data-driven decision. A formal method for collecting these data is required to ensure that your data are complete, consistent, clean, convenient, and controlled. It is only with properly gathered and organized data that we can make valid decisions using our data.

Improperly gathered and organized data can cause many issues with how we make data-driven decisions. Improperly collected data can not only make it impossible to answer our business questions, we may also not be able to defend the answers or test their validity. We may be able to answer a question, but that answer will be impacted negatively and provide a distorted view of the reality we are attempting to describe. This can cost the company money by acting on bad data. If the answers we derive from bad data are used to make bad decisions that can have a cascading negative impact on other decisions being made or can damage the trust others have in you and your analyses. Imagine a surgeon using bad data to decide on a course of treatment. You want your doctors to use valid data to make their decisions. Your data-driven decisions may not be life threatening, but they can feel that way to a company when they affect their bottom line.

Integrity must be maintained, regardless of where or how data are collected. Issues in the data collection process need to be addressed and solved as soon as they are detected, and any bad data corrected or eliminated in order to ensure that you are using the best and most valid data for your data-driven business decisions. The largest and most difficult issue for a company to overcome is the lack of a data culture within they workplace. If employees responsible for gathering and recording valuable data do not understand the value of those data, or have any concept of how even the most seemingly insignificant piece of information can impact the company and their success, those employees are not likely to take the necessary care in gathering that data. It is difficult to convince someone that a few extra clicks or filling in some additional fields is not a waste of their precious time. What would cost a user a few additional seconds could save or make the company money much more valuable than those few seconds of their time.

If there is such a concept as not enough data, there must be such a thing as too much data. I would expand that to say there is such a thing as not enough valid data and too much invalid data. Here lies another concept that may be difficult for the individuals gathering the data to appreciate. There is no such thing as too much valid data, but data that is not relevant or useful to the company may not be valid. If you do not work for the Department of Motor Vehicles, you probably are not needing to collect your customers' driver's license numbers. This is perfectly valid and useful data for the DMV but may not provide any meaningful information to a software company. By the same token, the users' computer operating system version might be critical for the software company but mean nothing to the DMV employees analyzing their data. This example is pretty obvious, but there is a wealth of data that can be collected that may be valid and useful, but on its surface appear to be merely trivial. Later I will speak to correlation and causation, but for now, consider that there are patterns that will only emerge if you have the data to expose them.

There are many humorous examples of meaningless correlations. One such correlation that you may practice yourself is the effect your socks have on the outcome of a sporting event. This example is a bit more like superstition, but if you have observed that your team is doing great this season and you happened to have been wearing the same socks for each game, you could fall victim to pareidolia. Pareidolia is the practice of observing random outcomes and imposing some sort of pattern on them. When we determine that a pattern does indeed exist using some mathematical testing and a much larger set of data, then we have an actual correlation that should receive our attention. Correlation does not prove anything other than of the countless variables in the world, we have found two that seem to follow a similar pattern. With more testing, we might declare that there is causation, but that takes a bit more work.

It may not be obvious to us as we are collecting data which of these data will have a relationship to other data, but we know that we will never discover something meaningful if we do not have the data to examine. We may find that certain products sell better to customers of a particular industry or we may detect a trend among minority-owned businesses in a particular region. I am fond of saying that we do not know what we do not know, and we cannot analyze data that we do not have. So clearly it is important to collect as much data as possible, or at least as much as makes sense. But how do we keep all of this data organized?

Organizing your data is as important as collecting it. After all, you can have all the data in the world, but if you cannot find it, it is of no value to you. Imagine trying to find this book in a library or bookstore if all of the books were just piled up in a heap with no order to them. A method for organizing things is critical in many aspects of our lives. As a father of two boys, I have observed that organization skill is definitely something that must be developed and taught. I currently have several large totes full of Lego™ bricks in my home, each containing thousands of bricks of all colors and sizes. These bricks began as organized sets designed to build a specific model, but quickly became a disorganized mess. Now if one of my boys wanted to build one of those models again, it would take hours of sorting through mountains of bricks to find the necessary pieces. As the boys have gotten older, they have gotten better at organization, but still fall victim to inherent laziness come laundry day when they regress to their earlier habits of making unorganized piles.

One way we manage to organize data is commonly called an ETL which stands for Extract, Transform, and Load. Data at their source is likely to be organized in a way that is not conducive to analysis. These data may be in tables that are designed for transactional work like sales or service, but not necessarily in the format or schema that would best work for consuming these data and making data-driven decisions. The ETL process is one that extracts the data from their sources, then through a series of written instructions or routines, reorganizes those data. Transformation may include many changes to the format, data types, and relationships within the data. The final step in the ETL process is to load the data into a database that can be used for analysis. ETL processes are also used to store backups of data and snapshots of data into a data warehouse.

Let's continue with the toy brick analogy for a moment. Suppose we wanted to get those bricks organized again and needed to come up with a method for doing that. The first step would be to determine how we plan to use the bricks after we have them organized. Will we be trying to rebuild the original models, or build models of our own design? If we are planning to build the original models, it probably makes sense to separate the bricks out into the necessary parts for each model. This is fine but does limit what we can do with the bricks, plus we are likely to have extras bricks or missing bricks – incomplete data if you will. I happen to know that some of those bricks were removed from my feet and thrown in the garbage in a fit of painful rage, so I suggest a different organizational scheme. We could separate the bricks by type, color, shape, and or size. If we start by segmenting the bricks from the little characters and specialty parts, then sort the other bricks by color and then within each color by type (flat, block, or angled perhaps), and then group bricks of similar color and type by size (number of posts on the surface, let's say) then we would have a pretty well-organized collection of bricks. It should be quite easy to find the bricks you need to build your model.

Now, after getting our bricks organized, what do we do with all of those bricks? We cannot leave them in piles on the floor and not expect them to be thrown out or get mixed or corrupted in some way. We need a way to keep them organized and some rules for how new bricks should be added to the collection. Rather than begin debating on the best way to store bricks, let's break from this analogy and discuss data storage.

You may not be familiar with databases, and that is okay. You do not need to be a database expert to be data-literate, but it is helpful to understand how databases organize data. Just like shelves at the library or bins for toy bricks, databases allow us to segment, group, and sort our data. Databases provide some rules for how data is stored and where data of different types should go. Usually, for the majority of employees in a company, they have no idea they are entering anything into a database or what that underlying database looks like. Most systems employees are using simply provide a user interface that presents forms (screens of fields) that the user completes and saves. When these data are written to the back-end database, each datum is stored as part of one or more record in the database. These records are grouped together, usually by type or subject. For instance, all account records are generally found on a table containing only account records. Depending on the database, the tables of records are probably related to one another so that you can identify the contacts on the contact table that belong with the account on the account table. This is done using a key that identifies the related record in the other table.

While this is not a book meant to teach you about databases, it is important that you add some information about databases to your knowledge bank. So, let's begin with what a database is. A database is a structured set of data stored in a computer's memory or in the cloud that organizes and makes data available in multiple ways. As we know, we are surrounded by data. Everything is data and data are everything we can see, or sense – they just need to be captured somehow. Companies use databases full of data about each of us in order to suggest products we may like, tell us which movies we are likely to enjoy, or what new music artists fits our taste. We see pop-up ads on our computers and receive coupons in the mail – usually not randomly, but by design based on data about us kept in massive databases.

To pull this off, they need to store data according to some structure. Databases provide this framework and rules for how data may be stored and retrieved. We all use databases today within our companies. We may not be using them to cyber stalk our customers yet, but we have them and want to use them to our advantage by providing ourselves with the data we need to make valid data-driven decisions.

There are two primary families of database. Relational databases are like the one I began describing above. In a relational database the data is organized and stored in tables that are linked to one another based on a relationship. Your company may have a database with all of your clients in a table and all of the contacts for those clients in another table. In the client table, each client is assigned an identifier that is unique and only used for that specific client. In the contacts table, you will have contact data which may also include a contact identifier. Along with each contact in the table, a client identifier will be included to define which client each contact is related with.

Understanding the relationships between entities allows us to better analyze our data and find similarities that may help us make better decisions about how we sell to or service our clients. This database keeps the data organized and tidy and much easier to maintain.

The other family of database are the non-relational databases. These may also be referred to as No-SQL databases. In these databases, the data are stored by category rather that relationship. Rather than use related tables to organize the data, the non-relational database will store all relations in a single document-like format where each set of data are assigned a unique key that ties all the data together. Adding data and updating data are still possible as long as you understand the format of the document. To someone unfamiliar, the data will likely look more like the software code of a program than a table with columns and rows.

These are referred to as no-SQL databases because as you may have inferred, one cannot use Structured Query Language (SQL) to access the data. SQL is sometimes pronounced "See-quill" so if you are ever asked if you know what "see quill" is, you can smile, nod, and say "ah yes, structured query language." SQL is probably the most popular language used to work with data in relational databases. It is very flexible, and allows the developer to add, update, and delete columns and tables and relationships with relative ease. Learning SQL is simple, and the syntax is easy to master. Using SQL, you can take advantage of the relationships between tables and get all of the data you need without repeating a lot of code for each table. Most, if not all, relational databases are built around SQL making it reliable and nearly universal.

You may be wondering why anyone would ever use a no-SQL database if the relational SQL databases are so powerful and easy to use. Believe it or not, there may be some instances where a no-SQL database makes sense to use. I will not go too deep on the topic of selecting the right type of database here as it is not likely that as someone who is reading this book, you are faced with this decision very often. The benefit of a relational database is in its simplicity of design. Every but of data belongs in a particular table and those tables are related so all of the data is reportable together. Unfortunately, because the relationships between tables are so critical, it sometimes is an issue when something break with these relationships, or one of the tables in the database is mistakenly dropped and needs to be restored. In a no-SQL database, all the related information is stored together in the same documents, so if one aspect of the dataset becomes corrupt, you are still able to work with all of the other aspects without loss of those data. If this tolerance is critical to your business, then you may tend toward a no-SQL solution over the consistency and ease of a SQL database.

If relational databases are made up of tables, it is important to understand exactly what a table is. At the risk of over-simplifying it, a table is just a grid of data made up of one or more columns containing one or more rows of data. Since nothing can ever be quite that simple, let's take our examination of a table a bit further. Suppose you are managing a youth bowling team. You have a roster of players that you are needing to keep organized. So let's start with a list of player names.

Player Name
Shawn
Sam
Dakota
Dallas
Steve
Cindi
Cassie
Robert

Each of your bowlers wears a particular size bowling shirt and uses a particular weight ball. You also want to track what their personal best game score is and their ages. So, let's expand our list and add some columns.

Player Name	Shirt Size	Ball Weight	Age	Best Score
Shawn	Large	14	13	185
Sam	Extra Large	16	14	176
Dakota	Medium	14	13	204
Dallas	Medium	12	13	199
Steve	Large	14	14	220
Cindi	Large	10	13	218
Cassie	Small	12	13	165
Robert	Extra Large	14	14	200

Now we have a table. This table is made up of rows with one row for each player. Rows may also be called "records" or "tuples" in a database. This table also contains columns with one column for each bit of information about the players. These may be called "attributes", "dimensions", or "fields" as well.

At this point we have a single flat table. This is a perfectly acceptable way to organize and store your data if your needs are relatively simple. If you are needing to store more information, you might create additional tables in a database with relationships identified between the table to help keep the data organized or segment the data for easier update and reporting. If so, the table will need to include a unique identifier that can be referenced in other tables to create these relationships.

Relationships in a database can be one-to-one, one-to-many, or many-to-many. A one-to-one relationship is where each record in one table is related to a single record in another table. Suppose we have a separate table in our database for contact information. That structure would look something like this:

PID	Player Name	Shirt Size	Ball Weight	Age	Best Score
P1	Shawn	Large	14	13	185
P2	Sam	Extra Large	16	14	176
P3	Dakota	Medium	14	13	204
P4	Dallas	Medium	12	13	199
P5	Steve	Large	14	14	220
P6	Cindi	Large	10	13	218
P7	Cassie	Small	12	13	165
P8	Robert	Extra Large	14	14	200

PID	Phone Number	Parent Name	Address
P1	(123)456-1111	Michael	100 First St.
P2	(123)456-2222	David	200 Second St.
P3	(123)456-3333	Susan	300 Third St.
P4	(123)456-4444	James	400 Fourth St.
P5	(123)456-5555	Kathryn	500 Fifth St.
P6	(123)456-6666	Joan	600 Sixth St.
P7	(123)456-7777	Robert	700 Seventh St.
P8	(123)456-8888	Daniel	800 Eighth St.

In this example, notice the addition of the player identifier (PID) column to the Player table and the Contact table includes a row for each unique PID from the Player table. This is what defines the relationship. As we continue to discuss database structure at a high-level, I want to introduce you to a common way database schema is illustrated. The above schema of two tables with a one-to-one relationship would appear something like this:

Players	
PID (PK)	INTEGER
Player_Name	TEXT
Shirt_Size	TEXT
Ball_Weight	INTEGER
Age	INTEGER
Best_Score	INTEGER

Contacts	
PID (PK)	INTEGER
Phone_Number	TEXT
Parent_Name	TEXT
Address	TEXT

This is not necessarily the best design, nor is it entirely necessary to have these data in separate tables in this example. There are many considerations when designing the schema for a database, and data modeling is not something that I intend to dig too deeply into with this book. You do not need to know how to structure the schema of a database, but to be data literate, it helps to have some idea of what is going on behind the scenes and understand how data are related within the databases you work with. Let's go on to look at a one-to-many relationship. In a one-to-many relationship each row in one table may be related to one or more rows in another table. One-to-many relationships allow you to store frequently used data in the parent table (the "one" side of the relationship) and reference this information many times in the child table (the "many" side of the relationship). In the child table there should be a foreign key, which is the primary key from the parent table. A good example of this might be table of scores for our players. We could structure this schema like this:

Players	
PID (PK)	INTEGER
Player_Name	TEXT
Shirt_Size	TEXT
Ball_Weight	INTEGER
Age	INTEGER
Best_Score	INTEGER

Scores	
ScoreID (PK)	INTEGER
PID (FK)	INTEGER
Game_Dt	DATE
Venue	TEXT
Score	INTEGER

PID	**Player Name**	**Shirt Size**	**Ball Weight**	**Age**	**Best Score**
P1	Shawn	Large	14	13	185
P2	Sam	Extra Large	16	14	176

Score ID	**PID**	**Game Date**	**Venue**	**Score**
1	P1	9/8/2020	AMF East	180
2	P1	3/19/2021	KingPins	176
3	P1	5/17/2021	AMF West	182
4	P2	3/19/2021	KingPins	170
5	P2	5/17/2021	AMF West	176

In the above excerpt from our fictional database, you see I was able to record multiple game scores for each player without needing to include all the player information multiple times. Only the PID which is the primary key for the Player table and the foreign key for the Scores table is repeated to identify which player goes with each score.

Now, let's imagine what the schema will look like if I need a many-to-many relationship. Let's pretend that as the Bowling coach you provide loaner equipment to your players and need to track which loaner items were borrowed each time. Since a player may borrow multiple items and each type of items can be borrowed by multiple players, we need a many-to-many relationship. Our Equipment table will have a primary key identifying each type of item (balls, towels, bag, brace, etc.) and the Transactions table will have a primary key identifying each transaction. But since each of these keys need to be referenced multiple times in each relationship, we must also include a third table to define the related records. This will be our EquipTrans table and will include the foreign keys (primary key from each of the parent tables).

Equipment	
EquipID (PK)	INTEGER
Name	TEXT
Quantity	TEXT

Transactions	
TranID (PK)	INTEGER
PID (FK)	INTEGER
Date	DATE

EquipTrans	
EquipID (FK)	INTEGER
TranID (FK)	INTEGER

With this schema we can see that the EquipTrans table contains only foreign keys. This table's sole purpose is defining the relationship between the equipment borrowed and the loan transaction. We are essentially building a many-to-many relationship by creating two relationships that are one-to-many or many-to-one depending on your vantage point. There is a one-to-many relationship between Equipment and EquipTrans. Each piece of equipment is identified once in the Equipment table and the EquipTrans table may contain many rows related to each row in the Equipment table. We also have a one-to-many relationship between Transactions and EquipTrans. Each transaction is recorded once in the transaction table, but the EquipTrans table may contain many references to each transaction. The EquipTrans table is the junction between the other two tables and is called the junction table. This may also be referred to as the mapping table or intermediary table.

Tables in our database may have multiple relationships to other tables. Look carefully at the Transactions table in this schema. Notice that there is a foreign key for the Players table. Each transaction is related to one player, so we have an additional one-to-one relationship here.

I would be remiss if I did not mention normalization here as we discuss relational database design. It is an advanced topic that gets into the refinement of database design and is therefore not required for most people to understand to be considered data literate, but it is common enough a topic that you might hear the terms bantered about in conversation between data science types who enjoy such intercourse.

Normalization allows for the manipulation and querying of data using a logical query such as SQL. Normalization is intended to simplify the individual tables and reduce the need for restructuring of the database when new relationships are introduced, or existing relationships removed. If a database has not been sufficiently normalized, errors may occur when attempting to insert, update, or delete records in the database. If an update were to cause duplicate information to appear on multiple rows, violating the uniqueness rule of the primary key, there will be an error. If attempting to insert a new row but a key field is not yet available there will be an error. If attempting to remove a row that breaks other relationships without also deleting data from other tables, there will be an error.

You may hear terms like First Normal Form and Second Normal form. Each level of normalization is defined according to how the database schema is set up. The goal of normalization is to reduce duplication of data and make the schema flexible enough to add to and remove from the schema without breaking anything. A database in a higher normalization form will have many small tables containing just lists of values and a key that is referenced in relationships. Tables are more likely to contain only single or a few dependent facts. For now, just know that if someone tells you that the data need to be normalized, they are indicating that the database tables should be split into multiple related tables.

Most databases should have the organizational schema documented in something called a data dictionary. A data dictionary documents the contents, format, and structure of the database. It also describes the relationships between elements in the data. A good robust data dictionary will include names and attributes of each datum and will define each so that the meanings and purposes of each data element are clear to the users of the data. The benefits of a data dictionary out-value the effort required to produce a good data dictionary. A good data dictionary will assist in avoiding data inconsistencies, particularly when there are multiple people providing those data. The data dictionary will define conventions that should be used when working with the data, and consistency in the collection of data. Well defined data is simply easier to analyze because you are not needing to work as hard to determine which data to use and how those data are formatted and related. Finally, a good data dictionary makes it much easier to enforce data standards. Data standards are the rules used to control the way data are collected, stored, retained, and used. If everyone complies with a set of standards, then everyone are good stewards of the data and the data maintains a level of credibility when scrutinized.

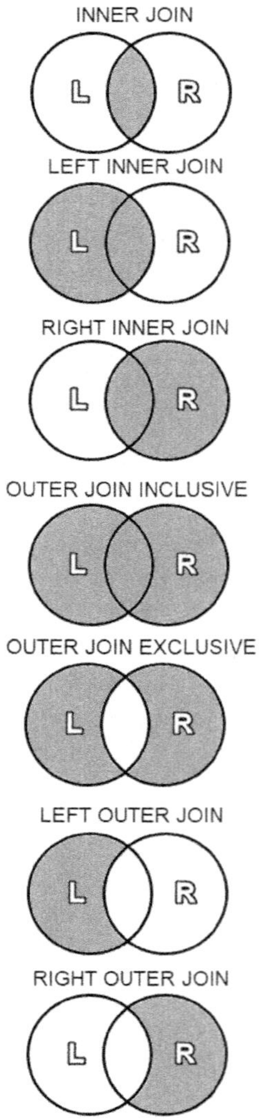

To retrieve data from a physical database, we construct a query that essentially asks the database to provide us data according to some defined filter requirements. The query will include which columns of data should be included from which tables and how those data should be organized in the result. The query result is not a physical object in the database. It is a logical operation that we use to access data that we may then save into a file or feed into a report. You may also encounter the concept of joins when querying data in a database or multiple databases. A join is a logical connection between datasets defined in the query to obtain a set of data in the result that is brought together in a union according to the parameters of the join. There are seven types of joins: inner, left inner, right inner, outer inclusive, outer exclusive, left outer, and right outer.

Inner joins will only retrieve data where a common value is present in both datasets. For instance, if you were to query a dataset that included books in a bookstore's inventory and a separate dataset with process for books, the result would give you a list of only the books in inventory for which there is a price noted. A left inner join on the same data will return all the rows that are common between the two (books in inventory that have a price) along with any other rows from the left side of the join. This would give us a list of all of our books in inventory but will only include prices that appear in the price dataset. Any book without a price will have a null (blank) value in the price field. The left table in this case is inventory because in my theoretical query I mentioned inventory before I mentioned pricing. If I wanted all the prices but only the inventory counts of the books on hand, I would use a right inner join.

An outer inclusive join keeps all data from both datasets and includes nulls where there is data not available for a particular row in one of the datasets. The result is essentially a combination of the left and right inner joins. No rows are excluded in a full outer inclusive join. An outer exclusive join eliminates the common elements from both datasets. In our example, this would include all books in inventory and all process except for those books in inventory with a price. A left outer join excludes common rows and all rows from the right dataset. This would give us all books in inventory for which there is no price. Finally, a right outer join excludes everything from the left dataset.

5
IDENTIFYING TYPES OF DATA

At the beginning of this book I discussed data as being qualitative or quantitative in nature and working at different levels of detail like ordinal, nominal, interval and ratio. One thing that you may find as you learn more about data is that there are many ways to describe and label different forms of data that it can be very confusing and hard to know when to use which description. I classified data previously into two areas: qualitative data and quantitative data. We classified qualitative data as being more conceptually descriptive and quantitative as being more metrically descriptive of some attribute in our dataset, speaking at a very high level. As we move into a deeper understanding of data, there are a few sub-classifications we can use to describe how that data behaves. You may also hear these called variable types. We will revisit variables later, so for now I will just refer to them as discrete, continuous, and categorical.

Quantitative data can be discrete or continuous. Discrete data is data that can have only certain values for a given attribute. A bowling ball comes in weights of 12, 14, 16 pounds. These are discrete because they are values from a fixed set of bowling ball weights. If, however, we were weighing these balls ourselves, and recording actual weight we might get 12.1, 14.45. 15.85 or any of an infinite number of weights depending on the precision of our scale. This type of data is Continuous. Another example may be shoe size. When you order shoes, you are ordering them according to a discrete measure of size. However, if you were to measure the length of many shoes of the same size, you will get many different lengths. The Size is discrete. Another way to think about discrete vs continuous discrete data is countable (how many bowler's use a 14lb. ball?) and continuous data is measurable (how much do we spend each month on bowling?). Let's jump ahead just a bit and think about how discrete data and continuous data might appear on a chart. Imagine we have collected all the ages and heights of students in a school. We are collecting a single measure of each child's height and weight and plotting them to the nearest inch in height and pound in weight. We would end up with a chart that looks something like this scatterplot.

If you selected a single child and plotted their weight over time as they aged, you would have similar data in that your datapoints are weight and age, but this data would be continuous as it changes over time. This chart would look quite different, and the points would follow a path rather than be scattered. That would look like this:

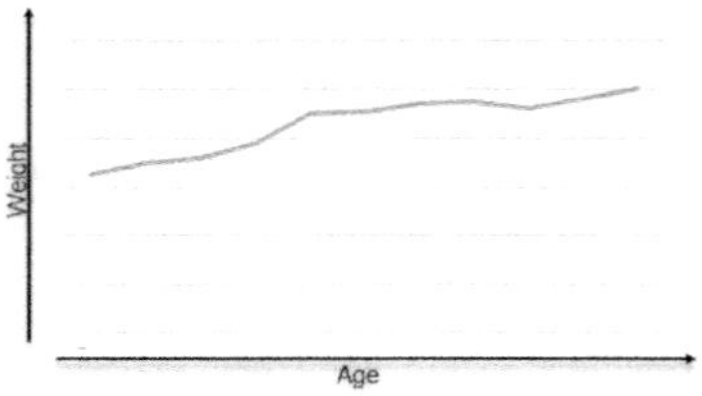

When we discuss visualizing data in a future chapter, this distinction becomes important because you can sometimes treat continuous data as discrete data depending on the type of question you are attempting to answer. Discrete data is data that you can tally, but sometimes you may want to count the number of times each value in a continuous data column appears in the data.

Within qualitative data, we have categorical data. Categorical data would be things that have a finite number of options that are not measures such as gender, race, product type, service team, etc. These data may be nominal or ordinal in nature and are the types of data we usually use to filter our analyses or define the contents of a study.

In the last chapter you became a bit more familiar with how we organize these data into a database, let's dive a bit deeper into the different types of data at the field level. Each column in a database is assigned a very specific data type and every value in that column in every row must adhere to that data type. Some are very specific, and others are rather loose in how they are defined, but strict adherence to the type assigned to each column is an absolute necessity.

If you were to ask multiple people familiar with data how many different data types are there, you would likely get several different answers. This is because different databases use different names and definitions of the data types used. When we get right down to it, however, we can group them all into strings, numbers, and dates/times. Variants within each of these groups provide us with the many data types you will encounter as you become data literate.

String data are made up of any combination of letters, numbers, or symbols that appear on your keyboard. Even if you only type numbers into a string field, the information is treated as text. The string data types are different according to the size (number of characters or bytes) the database will accept into the field. This can range from a single character Boolean type field or a character large object (CLOB) type field that can contain gigabytes of data.

Numeric data are made up of only numbers. The data type of numeric fields may indicate how the data is stored and displayed within the database. Integers or whole numbers are generally in a different number data type than are real or floating decimal numbers. Most databases allow you to set the precision and scale of floating decimal numbers where the precision is the total number of digits including both sides of the decimal, and scale is the number of digits after the decimal. For example, a number with a precision of 10 and scale of 4 would look like 123,456.1234. A number with a precision of 6 and scale of 6 would only have numbers to the right of the decimal such as .123456. There may also be some special number fields designed to handle currency figures.

Date and Time data are made up of numeric data that defines years, months, days, hours, minutes, and seconds sometimes down to the nanosecond. There are typically data types that include only the date, only the time, or both date and time. There are also some special timestamp data types that do not store data in any date format you may be familiar with and instead provides the time in a count of the number of seconds since the last epoch (Unix time) that began at 1970-01-01 00:00:00 UTC. This date was arbitrarily selected as the beginning of time by Unix programmers. It has been used ever since as a standard for recording time in computer programs.

Specific data type values for some common database languages are included in Appendix B for your reference. Knowing these specific types are not required to consider yourself data literate but understanding that there are differences in data types and that it is important to organize your data according to some rules and intended usage makes sense and will save you many headaches in the future when you are asked to interpret some data or expect a computer to interpret the value of something in your data.

The data type attribute tells the computer, the database software, and you how to interpret a value. Gathering and storing your data according to their data type is essential in ensuring that you have clean data and valid data as you begin your analysis. Suppose you are gathering some data via a paper form. The human writing information onto that form is not governed by data type or format. Numbers may be written with or without decimal places or rounded up or down. Dates may be written in any of a couple dozen ways. Month, day, year or year, month, day or day month year. Is 06-10-2021 June 10th or October 6th? Would you prefer 11:00 PM or 23:00? If the person completing the form just enters 11:00 it is not safe to assume that is 11:00 AM unless you have enforced some rule to include am or pm or enter time in military time (24-hour clock).

Suppose you are designing a survey and ask the respondent to rate something from 1-10 but neglect to inform them of which end of the scale is good and bad. What if you did not include an option of "not applicable" and not all respondents have an experience to rate. Average scores will certainly be skewed, and your results will be invalid. How do you interpret the blanks?

Using technology, data collection becomes a bit easier because we can add some guardrails like making some questions required and not allowing invalid entry, but we still need to pay attention to our data types and consider which data type will give us the quality of data we need while generating valid data with which we will make decisions. By using specific data types in our databases, we ensure that our data is consistent and with clean consistent data you are better able to provide real insight and make valid decisions.

Not all data types lend themselves to analysis. String data types are often much more difficult to consider in your analysis because the data is unstructured. There are limited rules governing what values may be entered or how long or short a value may be. Even if you limit string fields to a few hundred characters, you are still forced to work harder to extract meaningful data from these fields for analysis. You cannot control people's ability to spell, their use of acronyms and abbreviations, or even the correct word for what they are trying to say. Particularly in the last several years, I have seen more string fields populated with nonsense that may make sense in a social media comment or text message. While technology is working hard to catch up with natural language processing artificial intelligence, chances are you do not have access to such tools to work with your data.

If you are fortunate enough to be collecting your own data rather than using the data you are provided, then a knowledge of data types will help you gather the right sort of data needed to support your analysis. This luxury is not always available to us, so it is important to know what some of the limitations of different data types may be so you can either adjust your approach to the analysis or determine that analysis on the data you have available will not be reliable or valid enough to use in making data-driven decisions.

Over the next couple of chapters, we will discuss more about the quality of the data and how to limit the amount of bias in your data. For now, there are some particular attributes of some of the data types that I want to mention. I am assuming now that you are using a computer to perform your analysis, or the analysis you are reviewing was generated on a computer. It is interesting that as helpful as computers are, they are often a bit too rigid. If you are not aware of these potential pitfalls, you may find yourself wondering where you went wrong.

Let's start with an easy one. Integer fields store only whole numbers. If you add two integer fields together, your result will still be a whole number (12+5=17). If you subtract (12-5=7) or multiply (12*5=60), you will have a whole number result. The computer will not automatically change the data type of the result. It will always be a whole number. But what if we divide two integers? If I ask the computer to divide 12 by 5, it will try to return an integer. It might give us a 2 or depending on the program it might return a 1 or 0. As a human dividing two integers, we are not bound by the data type and know that the correct answer is 2.4. If you are not careful, you may not notice that this has happened and assume that the result is correct.

Another trap that is easy to fall into is with Boolean fields. These fields are often presented as a checkbox on a computer screen. Sounds simple enough. A check in the checkbox equals "yes" and probably puts a 1 in a field in the database. If the checkbox is not checked, that is "no" right? Well, not necessarily! A Boolean field, if not defaulted to a value of zero, has three potential states. Checked (1), unchecked (0), and never been checked (Null). If you were to do something like count all the positive responses (20) in your data and divide that by the number of records (100) to arrive at a percentage of positive responses, you would get a result of 20% positive. This does not necessarily mean that you have 80% negative. What if only 25% of your users (25) gave an answer by clicking on the checkbox for a positive response (20) or clicking on the checkbox and then clicking it again to remove the check for a negative response (5)? Now you can report that of 100 users, 20% are positive and 5% are negative and 75% did not answer. You could also claim that of the respondents who answered (25) you have 80% positive and 20% negative. We will come back to the decision on which of these correct statistics is the most appropriate to use in your report.

I mentioned the data and time fields earlier. This is one that goes beyond just format though. When you are using a computer system to gather date data, it is important for you to know how the data are being stored and how the data are being presented back to you through the system or through a data extract. Let's say you are a sales manager on the west coast of the United States. You enter a record into the system, you are obviously going to see your local time in the Create Time field according to your home time zone. However, on the back end behind the scenes, the date and time is likely stored in a Universal Time Code. 12:00 becomes 19:00 in the database because the Pacific time zone is UTC-7. Now let's say I go in and look at that record from my office on the east coast. I would probably see that it was created at 3:00 pm because the system is showing me what is in the database (19:00) in my local time zone. Eastern time is UTC-4. All of this is great for users using the system. Chances are, if a user runs a report in the system, they will see times translated to their local time as well. What may or may not get translated from UTC is a data extract or download from the system to a flat file. Perhaps you have an analytics tool integrated with your system and it pulls data directly from the database. I know some systems also generate reports with times translated to the server time zone or the time zone of the company headquarters. None of this is an issue as long as you are aware of how times are being handled in the data and can perform the necessary conversions for your intended audience if appropriate to do so.

String fields of any type are usually more difficult to work with, but qualitative data is very important in most analysis of business data. If you are fortunate, the string fields you are using are populated through a provided list of values. If so, the data in those fields are consistent and probably spelled correctly. Watch out for "other" and similar worthless values. Those can skew your analysis significantly, so if you see that this is an option, you will want to carefully examine how those data are collected and ensure that you are able to derive some value from the field.

Sometimes, usually to avoid free-form text, the database designer has decided to allow for a multiple select field. These fields let the user select more than one value. These data are usually stored in the database field as a delimited list. For instance, if asked to select your favorite colors in a multi-select string field with a drop-down list, and you click on Blue, Red, and Green, the value stored in the database for that field might be "blue;red;green." This can be a nightmare if you are trying to query the data to see how many people selected "green" as one of their favorite colors. You cannot use a simple Colors field equals green filter, because that will only return the rows where "green" was the only color selected. You instead will have to search for rows where that field contains "green" to get the right results. This is usually not a problem unless you have a very large dataset, as this type of query tends to take longer to return results.

Another issue I sometimes have with the multi-select fields is in exporting the data from the database for some analysis. Often times the delimiters in the field will be interpreted by the .CSV or .XLS file I am pushing data into as multiple columns rather than a single column with multiple values. In order to be able to work with data from this type of field, I usually have to perform some transformations on the data to split the multi-select field out into a separate column for each value or normalize the data somehow depending on my goal. I would rather work with a multi-select field than a free-form text field any day, but care must be taken to maintain data integrity.

Some string fields allow for an enormous amount of text. These often times show up in applications as a Notes field or Description field. They also tend to get truncated in reports and extracts resulting in some data loss. There just is not any great way to use this type of data without some sophisticated AI tools, and I don't recommend attempting it without such tools. If you are ever asked to perform any sort of analysis using data from large string fields, it will be important for you to explain why you are unlikely to derive anything meaningful from these data.

I will conclude this chapter with this. You can be data-literate without knowing the data type details provided in Appendix B, but you cannot be data-literate without understanding the link between string data, number data, and date data types and the business question you seek to answer or decision you are asked to make. Data types provide many of the guard rails needed to have Complete, Consistent, Clean, Convenient, and Controlled data. Database rules along with data types will help ensure that your data is complete but remember that there may be null values lurking about. Data types will keep things consistent and clean, except for those pesky unstructured string fields. Performing analysis on data that is convenient and understandable and controlled using your knowledge of data types and how your data are collected is much easier thanks to a defined set of data types. One thing data type do not have much control over is the quality of your data selection or the bias that may be introduced as you work with data to make your data-driven decisions. That is what we will discuss next.

6
JUDGING THE QUALITY OF DATA

Not all data are useful for making data-driven business decisions. In fact, some data are very much the opposite and can lead you to some terrible data-driven decisions. Yes, even if it is a bad decision, if you relied on data to inform that decision, it is still data driven. I briefly introduced the V.A.L.I.D. model previously. This model will help us identify data that is valid for making data-driven decisions. Using the V.A.L.I.D. model along with the five Cs identified earlier, we will be on our way to working with quality data.

The V.A.L.I.D. model is going to give us a framework for selecting the best data to support data-driven decisions. One thing you will notice is that it is very difficult to identify how any data could ever adhere to one of the five points in the model without meeting the standards described in the other four. Invalid data is usually by its nature in violation of at least three of these rules. When one rule is broken it usually causes the rest to be broken as well. We will begin by further enhancing our understanding of how each of these points affects the quality of our data and the decisions we make from understanding those data.

The first point in the model is Verifiable. Valid data will come from a verifiable credible source. You do not want to be making workplace decisions based on data that you cannot trust. Any data you use should be endorsed by your company or in the case of publicly available data, come from a place you feel is providing reliable data. If you are using any sources of data to aid with your analyses or planning, be sure you provide a citation for where those data came from. This is not only good form, it allows others to make a judgement about how they want to use or trust those data and the results of your analysis. I suspect that most often, you will be working with data that is owned and provided by your employer. In this case, you still want to perform some due diligence to ensure that you fully understand how those data are generated, which people and systems may manipulate those data in some way, and that the data you are provided is either the complete dataset or a valid subset of that dataset. Understanding how data have been filtered and prepared before it gets to you is vital as you make data-driven decisions. You want to avoid working with a sub-set of data that you believe represents the whole dataset. It may be perfectly valid to work with a filtered set of data if your analysis is focused on a particular subset. If you are comparing 2020 to 2021, you probably do not need data from 2019 cluttering up your analysis. You do need to ensure, however, that no other unnecessary filters are being used and it is very clear which calendar you are using (in cases of fiscal calendars not matching year calendars) and which date field is being used for the filter. Collecting a mass of records filtered based on Sold Date when you want data filtered based on Created Date will likely send you in the wrong direction. The larger the dataset, the more difficult this type of error is to detect if you do not look closely.

Another situation where "verifiable" is important is survey data. If you are conducting a survey to gather the opinions of customers about a product, you are going to want to send that survey to customers who own and use the product. This may seem obvious, but I cannot tell you how many times I have been asked to rate my satisfaction with a company or product that I have never heard of. Surveys are tricky, because we know that you must send a ton of them out to get enough responses to mean anything, but this can lead to a lot of surveys going to people who may not provide valid results. I also question the validity of any survey that offers me a gift or payment for my opinions. That is just asking for invalid data. Some will answer more favorably perhaps because they really like the idea of getting that gift card. Some will answer blindly just to get the gift card. If you do a lot of work with surveys, I encourage you to research the psychology and science behind survey design. It is a much deeper subject than I can include here, and it is fascinating how the results can provide great insights and can be misleading depending on the bias, which is often unintentional and other times very intentional. This is why "Avoids Bias" is the second point in the V.A.L.I.D. model.

Bias may be introduced in your data in many ways and at many points during the process of collecting, organizing, examining, interpreting, and visualizing your data. There are many different types of bias that can affect your data-driven decision making. The next chapter will have you taking a deeper look at some of the many ways data and analyses may exhibit bias. Some biases affect the data directly like selection bias and exclusion bias. Others are introduced by the individuals or computer models working with the data such as over and under fitting, measurement bias, or communication bias. Your target audience may also bring their own biases to the data such as confirmation bias. Regardless of the type of bias or the source of the bias, it is important that you keep a careful eye on how bias may affect your data.

Biased data is usually not "Legitimate" as the next point in the model demands. Legitimate data will be able to support any claims that are made using those data and will need to be statistically relevant in order to do that. If our data collection process is poorly managed and we have a lot of dirty data and errors, we should not make data-driven decisions using those data. We also need to ensure that any conclusions to which we arrive is based on data that has a strong relationship to the variable we are testing for. In short, we need legitimate data to perform a legitimate analysis to reach a legitimate outcome.

Data that are valid for making data-driven decisions must be interpretable. If you or your audience do not understand what the data represents, don't rely on it to make decisions. The data you use should be easy to understand and have an obvious relationship to the question you are seeking to answer. A student's standardized test score has nothing to do with their ability to play chess. Sure, you could posit that a student of greater intelligence as shown by the test score would have a better chance at becoming a skilled chess player, but you will need to do a lot more work to support that argument. If we look at this same example from another angle, we may find that the average test score of chess players is higher than average score of students who do not know how to play chess. This is a good example of the correlation not proving causation. Just because there is a positive correlation here, there is no proof of causation. You cannot identify good chess players according to test scores, and you cannot increase test scores by teaching someone to play chess.

The goal of data literacy for the workplace is making good data-driven decisions based on valid data. If your data are not decisional and cannot be relied on for making decisions and justifying those decisions and measuring the benefit of those decisions, then you are making bad decisions and wasting your time with pointless analyses. When you are judging the quality of your data, ensuring that you are working with valid data is just the first step. Your data may seem to exhibit all of the elements of valid data, but still be of questionable quality. Identifying the best data to answer your question is only half the battle. Ensuring that those data are complete, consistent, clean, convenient, and controlled will mean we are using quality data as well as valid data when making data-driven decisions. Let's review the five Cs.

The 5 Cs are Complete, Consistent, Clean, Convenient, and Controlled. Quality data will be all of these, and each affects the quality of the data-driven decisions you will make using your data. Earlier we talked about these attributes referencing more the physical qualities of data. In this chapter we will be discussing some other qualities that may be less obvious. I also introduced the V.A.L.I.D. model that says data should be Verifiable, Avoid bias, Legitimate, Interpretable, and Decisional. This model speaks more to the validity of data and how you use those data to make valid data-driven decisions.

You will obviously want your data to be complete, but just because all the blanks are filled in, do not assume your data is complete. One of the easiest mistakes to make is not using enough data to develop a complete understanding before making a decision using those data. If you are trying to determine how seasonality affects sales, you must use more than one cycle through the seasons to identify that there is a consistent trend affected by seasonality. Generally, more data is always better. A larger dataset will provide more accurate results that are subject to less bias than a smaller set of data. Data will ideally be complete in the sense that all the potential data are included. For instance, if you are trying to determine the opinion of your customers but you only collect data from your long-standing happy customers who you already know will provide a more favorable viewpoint than other customers, you are not using complete data and your results will be biased. This is actually a strategy that we see employed all the time to support one position over another during political and moral discourse. As a data scientist, I will never endorse manipulating data selection or how data are examined to arrive at a pre-determined result, but no one can deny that it happens frequently. It is a dangerous and sometimes criminal mistake to make in the workplace. We want our data to be complete in the sense that is meets the requirement of validity, and we want our data to be complete in the physical sense as well. A column full of blanks or incomplete values is not helpful.

Consistency is a key quality of good data, and consistency is also important in your data collection methods, your approach to examining data, the way you define key metrics, and your communication of results. Consider a long-term study or comparison of year-over-year trends and other such analysis where you are comparing results of one dataset or time period with that of another. I have been asked a business question like this many times. How does this year's results compare to those from previous years? A perfectly reasonable request as long as the data is consistent in structure and collection methodologies. If the metrics you are looking to compare are affected by some change in process or due to a reorganization that took place within the company, they may lose some validity. At the very least, any inconsistencies between the datasets should be disclosed along with the results of your analysis. You might also consider a different business question that enquires about the effects of a change that occurred.

Clean data is very helpful and often an absolute necessity when working with data to make good decisions. We previously discussed this point regarding the actual cleanliness of the data values in the dataset. Poor spelling, incomplete values, odd characters, and bogus data values are attributes of data that needs to be cleansed. I can think of some other applications of the adjective in making data-driven decisions and communicating those decisions. I touched on it as a violation as completeness of data, and I am not going to preach to you about your personal moral compass here, but as data literate persons, there is a responsibility to be transparent and honest with data. As a statistician, it is quite easy to use data to support any particular position by picking and choosing the data I use or the visualizations I select to illustrate the results. I consider this to be very poor form and an unclean practice. The severity of unclean practices with data ranges from trivial to criminal, but if you are unsure, always err on the side of transparency so that others may form their own judgements of what value they give the data in order to make their own data-driven decisions.

Convenient in the 5 Cs model references the ability for people to access data in order to perform some analysis, but it can also apply to making the results accessible for others who may not be as data-literate as you. Transparency about how decisions were made, the data used, and the methodologies used gives others a better understanding of the decisions, makes them convenient to use and support. One way we make data convenient is in the way we present that data as we justify our decisions. This book does not intend to teach you how to create data visualizations, but to be data-literate, you will need to understand many of the strategies for visualizing data and most importantly, how to understand and use the visualizations created by others. With that bit of knowledge, however, you should find creating your own visualizations quite easy if you have the tools to do so.

Finally, controlled data is not just data that is well governed and maintained, but also can be applied to testing. If you are involved in analyzing test data, you will want to be sure that the results are from a valid test conducted in a controlled environment to avoid bias and inaccurate results. As you identify the data you want to evaluate to make business decisions, be sure that you are using data that is subject to some sort of data governance. If the quality of your data can be questioned due to the lack of control in collecting and using those data, then the validity of your data-driven decision can also be questioned. Imagine if you are denied a benefit promised for meeting a goal, but the method of tracking progress toward that goal consists of some poorly designed and regulated process such as an administrator remembering to update the spreadsheet that is kept on a shared network drive. There is very little control in how the administrator receives the information or records it. There is no security enforced on who can update the file, or how that file can be accessed. Without controls, the data may not be trusted, and decisions may be questioned.

Data quality in today's business environment has become the responsibility of every position in the company. Your business needs to ensure that everyone has access to quality valid data. You cannot rely on a small group of people to maintain all the data. The IT department can only do so much and likely does not have the domain knowledge to completely judge the quality of the data. A small data science team can certainly provide some advice and guidance but cannot be responsible for things outside their control like data entry or network security. If everyone in your company has an understanding, or at least appreciation of the importance of quality data, then the people generating your data and collecting and controlling that data can take on some of the responsibility for data quality. The salesperson who can recognize that complete data allows for data-driven decisions that will greatly benefit sales is more likely to take the extra few moments to fill in all of the fields on the screen or do the research necessary to collect the most accurate data.

If your company values data as an asset, then they are likely investing in the data in a number of ways to enhance the quality. Systems can usually be automated with checks of rules for data. Enforcing formats and making key fields required can feel like a nuisance to someone entering data without an appreciation for the value of quality data. Often companies will take steps to enrich their data by supplementing the data entry with data from other sources that may fill in many of the blanks. Quality data is not something that is completed only once. Monitoring the quality of data must be an ongoing effort so data remains current and correct over time. Valid, high-quality data can benefit you and your company in a great way both financially and in the growth of your business. Poor-quality unhealthy data can cost you and your company success. This is why it is so important that quality data be used to make data-driven decisions, and you are able to recognize data that should and should not be used to make those decisions.

7
DETECTING BIAS

Bias is a bad thing. You have probably been taught this since the time you could first make a decision. If you have been a parent more than a few years, you have heard "that's not fair" more times than you can count. There is little doubt that you have been the victim of some sort of bias at some point in your own life. Your decision to buy this book was probably biased in some way. The point is, bias is bad, but it is nearly impossible to avoid. Even when evaluating data, bias is there affecting that evaluation and potentially impacting your data-driven decisions. While the goal to eliminate all bias from the world is perhaps the loftiest goal of all, it is reasonable to eliminate as much bias as you can when working with data in the workplace.

If you immediately thought of racism or ageism or gender bias or any of the social discrimination biases when you began reading this chapter, you already understand that bias is based on some moral code of fairness and equality. Bias in data is similar, but a great deal more nuanced. In the most general sense, bias is a prejudice toward or against one thing compared to another. When speaking about bias in data, we define different types of bias based on how we identify, observe, collect, use, measure, and communicate data. It has come up in previous chapters that more data is better than less data and using the wrong data can impact results either for the better or the worse, and sometimes that is used to one's advantage to support an argument. My goal for this chapter is to help you detect and recognize bias so that you can eliminate it as much as possible rather than use it to fabricate your results.

If you asked multiple experts to list the different types of bias that one may encounter in data, you would get multiple lists that include different names for each. There is no one definitive list of agreed upon values in the set. Similarly, there is no single agreed upon classification of groups of biases. This is probably due to the tendency for one bias to lead to another or similarities between the bias types. If I were to group the biases by some sort of bias family, I would get something like confirmation biases, selection biases, exclusion biases, measurement biases, and communication biases. As you will soon see, there are some gray areas that blur the lines between some of the bias types. Each of these families contains multiple specific biases that describe how you or something in the data affects the level of truth supported by the data.

Confirmation biases are created by human nature. We are imperfect beings, and we have an innate need to succeed at everything we do. We simply want things to go our way. When we allow confirmation biases to affect our decisions, we are in some way interpreting results to meet some pre-conceived expectation. We often do this subconsciously, and we almost always have some sort of confirmation bias in every decision we make. One way we inject confirmation bias is through a biased search for information. When we are looking for information to use in decision making, we have a tendency to find more information that supports our viewpoint or expectation. Consider how you search the Internet for information. If you tend to think coffee is better than tea, you will likely search "is coffee better than tea?" and the search engine would obediently provide you with many links that will help you justify coffee's superiority over tea. If you were to search "is tea better than coffee?" the search engine will again take your side and provide plenty of data on tea being superior to coffee. When working with data in the workplace, you may subconsciously only ask for data from sources that you trust will support your viewpoint or benefit you in some way. It is easy to conveniently ignore some data that might be troublesome when you are making your argument.

Biased interpretation is another example of confirmation bias. Given evidence that can both support and oppose your viewpoint, you are likely to interpret that evidence to support your view. If I love tea and hate coffee, I will interpret your reasons for coffee being better in a different way than a coffee lover would. Think about the last "too close to call" action in a sporting event that you witnessed. If your team winds up with the penalty, you probably formed some negative opinion of the official making the call. If the other team gets the penalty, you may think that the official is the best there is. Even after watching a replay in slow motion, some fans will not accept that the call was correct if it does not favor them to do so. I see this a lot in the workplace in a couple different forms. Sometimes data is interpreted in a way that favors the interpreter by providing some justification as to why the data is more important or should be weighed more heavily that other data. It is also common for people to warp the meaning of data to suit themselves. If a phone rep has longer call times that other reps, you may assume they are having more meaningful conversations with customers or building a rapport with prospects. One could just as easily interpret long call times as inefficient, slow, or maybe they are talking with their friends rather than customers. The point is, if there is no standard definition of what is good or bad, we tend to provide one that suits us.

Biased recall is also an issue within confirmation bias. When asked to recall information that we have examined, we are more likely to remember the information that means more to our agenda than information opposing our viewpoint. This is also why timeliness of decision making is important. Making decisions using data that was analyzed and interpreted in the past based on how you remember it, it likely to introduce some recall bias into the decision. We also tend to recall extremes more readily than information that is more moderate in results. Think about your childhood. Do you recall the days when nothing unusual happened? You likely remember traumatic events and very joyful events quite easily. The same holds true with data. We tend to focus more on the extremes when recalling information, and we prefer to remember the joyful stuff rather than the traumatic.

Confirmation bias, also referred to as observation bias, is easier to detect in others than it is ourselves. This makes it important to consider how data is collected, interpreted, and remembered when evaluating a data-driven decision. It is also important that you provide a level of transparency to your analyses and decisions so that others can consider the effects of confirmation bias on your results. A distinction that should be made here is that confirmation biases tend to occur after you know something about the data. Selection bias can occur as the data is selected with or without knowledge of the data. It is a fine line, that is easily blurred.

The next family of biases to consider are selection biases. As bias families go, this is the largest. Selection bias is introduced when some of the data that could affect the results of an evaluation are lost or missed or simply never used. In statistical analysis of large datasets this can include how the data are sampled from the population. In statistical studies we are taught to use random sampling to avoid bias. A truly random sample is not always easy to come up with.

Sampling bias is an error of not using a random sample, or not using a dataset where some portions of the data are less likely to be included than others. One way to avoid sampling bias is to not use a sample. If you can reasonably include the entire population of data in your analysis, you need not be concerned with a sample that does not properly represent the population. If you are working with an analysis of sales performance for the entire company, then it may be possible to use the entire population for your analysis. What you would not want to do is to examine the data from one sales office location and claim that those results are representative of the entire company. There are other times when sampling bias is simply impossible to avoid. Take a customer survey as an example. If you send a survey to every customer, you will probably feel pretty good about getting a third of them completed and returned. That entire set of survey data only represents a portion of the population, but can it be considered an unbiased sample? No, because you did not randomly select from the population, the sample selected themselves. This is also called volunteer bias or self-selection bias. The results are biased because they only represent the portion of the population with a propensity toward completing the survey. If you offered a free gift for completing the survey, you are also biased toward customers who are motivated by gift cards. Pre-screening is another way to introduce selection bias. Consider the statistics you may see on a political candidate's advertisements. Do you think they surveyed all political parties evenly, or only called the people registered with their party? I suspect they performed a little pre-screening to find the people with opinions they want to include in their data. If your company sends out customer satisfaction surveys, do they only send them to customers who have never submitted a service ticket? Probably not, but if you suspect that they have, would you trust the results?

Time interval bias is when you select a period of time to represent a larger period of time. For instance, if I wanted to track an increase in the purchase of pencils, and only examined data from July and August to arrive at some conclusion, I will likely get results that do not reflect the whole and might increase my pencil inventory only to see sales plummet after the back-to-school rush is over. I see this argument used in society often on topics of climate change or economies. Selecting a favorable time period to make a point is biased. In addition to time period selection, one should also consider timeliness of the data. If data are old, they may no longer be relevant to current time decisions. This is particularly true in the technology sector where the landscape changes through innovation almost daily.

Exposure bias is an interesting one to look for in the workplace. It most often is seen in blind focus groups or jury selection. If you want your data to reflect a first impression or unbiased opinion of just the information presented, you are going to want to collect that data from a source that has not been pre-exposed to the information. Another potential source of exposure bias, which could be more common in the workplace, is exposure to the fact that the group is being watched. If you are collecting data through some observation of employee behavior or productivity in an effort to gauge the effectiveness of an intervention, you are likely to get some slightly biased results. People tend to perform differently when they know someone is watching and collecting data on their performance. In order for the data collected under observation to be unbiased, the observation needs to be a constant thing rather than a temporary variable. This is why managers actively involved with their employees tend to get the best results – or at least that is a good hypothesis that could be studied.

Self-selection bias, which we mentioned before, can also be an issue with selection bias when you are relying on participants to volunteer data. If you target certain participants knowing that they will give you the result you want, that is confirmation bias, but if you request participation from a large group and allow the participants who want to participate to select themselves for the study, then you will likely have a biased selection. This is particularly true if the subjects are aware of the study and its goals. This attention bias is introduced when the participants are aware of the attention being placed on them is called the Hawthorn effect. More on this in the section on Measurement bias.

Exclusion bias sounds like the opposite of selection bias, and in some ways, it is, but we are not excluding data based on bad sampling, but on the actual values within the data themselves. Much of the discussion around the necessity for complete and clean data hints toward exclusion biases. When data is not usable because it is not valid or uninterpretable, it should be excluded. Unfortunately, excluding too much data can affect your results and introduce a bias.

If we consider the normalized (bell) curve that you typically see with a large dataset, you will see that data measurements have a tendency towards the center. In other words, most of the datapoints are going to fall within the first standard deviation from the mean (average). Wait! Don't put the book down. I promise this is not a lesson in statistics. Now picture what you would have if you tallied the number of times a value appears in a large dataset that is measuring something like sales per salesperson. You would eventually have a shape that looks a bit like a bell. It might be a wide bell or a narrow bell, but the peak of that curve will be near the average, or if plotted using some statistics, it would be exactly the average. Now imagine that included in your dataset you have some values that are far outside the norm, some fields that have no values in them, and some other datapoints that just don't need to be there because of some other issue with their validity. When one of these situations exist, your data can get skewed in one direction or another.

Consider this… you are in a conference room with a dozen people. Each person in the room makes a salary between $100,000 and $200,000 each year. The average salary is around $150,000. Now, a billionaire walks into the room. The average salary just jumped to $200,000,000 a year. Does this mean that the typical person in this room is a millionaire? Of course not. The billionaire is an outlier. While it is mathematically accurate to say that the average salary in the room is $20,000,000 it is not useful information because it is misleading. In this case you probably want to exclude the outlier or use a different measurement to describe the salaries in the room, even though excluding data does introduce some bias, it may be the lesser of the biases encountered when including the data. If I were performing this analysis, I would likely offer the average salary without the outlier factored in, and the median (middle when ordered by size) salary including the outlier. Often the median is a more appropriate measure because it is less impacted by outliers than average. Here's the proof:

Person	Salary	Running Average	Running Median
1	$ 100,000		
2	$ 100,000	$ 100,000	$ 100,000
3	$ 120,000	$ 106,667	$ 100,000
4	$ 120,000	$ 110,000	$ 110,000
5	$ 150,000	$ 118,000	$ 120,000
6	$ 150,000	$ 123,333	$ 120,000
7	$ 160,000	$ 128,571	$ 120,000
8	$ 170,000	$ 133,750	$ 135,000
9	$ 170,000	$ 137,778	$ 150,000
10	$ 180,000	$ 142,000	$ 150,000
11	$ 190,000	$ 146,364	$ 150,000
12	$ 200,000	$ 150,833	$ 155,000
13	$ 2,600,000,000	$ 200,139,231	$ 160,000

average salary before billionaire enters
average salary including the billionaire
median salary before billionaire enters
median salary including the billionaire

So now let us continue with the same initial room of 12 people. Suppose we add a few people but do not know their salaries. Now we must decide how we want to describe the salaries in the room. If we keep the null values in this case, but include the three people in our calculations, the average salary of the 15 people now in the room drops to $120,667. If we exclude the three nulls, the average remains $150,883 but does that accurately describe the average salary of the room? We have no way of knowing because of the missing data. I have seen different strategies used in cases like this. Some advocate for assigning the average of the other values in place of each of the other values. This will not change the average, but also may not reflect reality. You must decide how much bias or error you are comfortable with. The larger the dataset, the less the impact of missing values. The outliers and nulls become sort of confounding variables.

Most analysis consists of independent and dependent variables. The independent variable is the thing that is changing, and you are interested in how that change relates to or causes changes in another measure. The dependent variable is the thing that may or may not change when the independent variable changes. Let's say you are interested in the sales performance based on tenure of your sales staff. The performance is the dependent variable (effect) and the tenure is the independent variable (cause). Your hypothesis is that as tenure increases so does sales performance. But wait, as tenure increases, so does the number of vacation days each employee is allowed. This third variable may impact both the independent and dependent variable in some unknown way and is therefore a confounding variable. Also, the newer salespeople are spending a large amount of time in training rather than selling. There is another confounding variable. Confounding variables can either inflate or deflate results. Regardless of if the confounding variables are positive or negative, they still introduce bias to your results and should be eliminated as much as possible. To eliminate the vacation days confounding variable, you might consider totaling the number of work days for each salesperson and calculating results accordingly rather than just blindly selecting a year or certain number of months as your date parameters.

My favorite group of biases are the measurement biases. They are not favorite because they are better or worse than any of the other ways bias affects data, but I really just love the phenomenon of math. I will begin with one that made my life as a training consultant and performance consultant a few decades ago a little more interesting. Attention bias, also called the Hawthorn effect, is bias that is introduced because people tend to perform differently when they know someone is paying attention. It was first defined when a company called Hawthorn Works had a study conducted to see if people worked more effectively at higher or lower levels of light. First, they turned the lights up, and productivity on the factory floor increased, but eventually returned to the baseline over time. Then they turned the lights down and productivity on the factory floor once again increased for a bit before returning to baseline. They tested other changes in the work environment and each time productivity temporarily increased. They eventually concluded that it was not the changes in the environment causing changes in performance. The changes occurred because the workers knew they were being watched. This is considered a measurement bias because your measurements are skewed not because of the independent variable, but because those being evaluated were providing data that would not ordinarily be provided. Combating this bias is sometimes as simple as hiding the fact that you are temporarily collecting data for analysis. Another method would be to time the analysis such that you are measuring short-term and long-term effects separately to allow for the Hawthorne effect. I mentioned that this bias made things interesting as a training and performance consultant. It actually worked to my advantage at times because any training or intervention I gave my client always appeared to be effective, and as a consultant, I was long gone before the performance returned to baseline. This phenomenon is similar to the placebo effect that makes ineffective drugs seem to work. This must be why medial studies are usually completed over a lengthy period.

Verification bias can be seen in instances where there is no single standard to verify results against. In the workplace we often have key performance indicators (KPIs) that are tracked and measured and used to judge success of employees. If the standard expected for a KPI is variable across the groups measuring against it, then any verification of results is potentially valued differently. One group could be considered successful because they met the KPI requirement while another group fails to meet the KPI requirement because the standard for the second group was higher than it was for the other group. If you are publishing results that compare performance against a standard, be sure everyone is using the same standards.

Equation bias occurs when the math being used to aggregate and report results is used incorrectly. With modern tools, this happens less than before, but we are still guilty of asking our computers to perform some math functions that do not give us the results we need because we asked for the wrong math. I find this happening in spreadsheet applications frequently. Regardless of how the equation is solved, there are certain rules of mathematics that must be adhered to. You may remember learning order of operations in math class in school. That order has not changed. Six minus two times three (6-2*3) is zero. It is not twelve. If you solved that problem in your head and got twelve as your solution, you neglected to follow the correct order of operations. You should multiply before you subtract so the problem becomes six minus six after completing the multiplication step. Where things get tricky is when the math problem is not presented in a neat little equation. In the workplace, we may have situations where we need to do some calculations and need to understand how the context affects the way the math is performed. Let's say you have a campaign that you have invested $6,000 into. If a client participates in the campaign, they receive your product for $2,000. This campaign generated 3 sales. How much did you make from this campaign? This is similar to the equation above ($6k - $2k * 3 sales) and you netted $0. Now, let's say you have 3 people each have $6, and each buy a $2 hotdog for lunch. How much money do they have if they pooled their money? Same numbers, different order. In this case you are subtracting the $2 from the $6 that each person has, leaving each of them with $4. There are three people, so their total remaining cash is $12. Context is important when designing any sort of calculation. Another common problem is averaging averages. This creates what is called Simpson's paradox. More on that later, but for now, just know that you should not take an average of averages and assume that represents the overall average.

There is another type of measurement bias that usually occurs within the statistical models of machine learning processes. Briefly, machine learning uses computer algorithms that can adjust themselves based on prior results. A model is designed and trained using known results, which allows the model to predict future results based on this training data. This process gives the computer the appearance of learning. The learning is limited because the business context is usually vastly more complex that what can be programmed into the artificial intelligence model. If the model is not monitored and adjusted accordingly, the model may begin to introduce bias through overfitting or underfitting. Overfitting occurs when the model corresponds so closely with one set of data that is may fail to fit other data properly. If a model is trained on a specific set of data, it may not know how to handle other data that does not follow the same patterns of the training data. Underfitting occurs when the training data does not give the model enough information and it is unable to reliably predict anything for any set of data due to poor training and lack of context.

Finally, we come to a set of biases that are the easiest to create because they are all about how you, as a data-literate person, read and interpret data and subsequently share those data with others. Most people using data in the workplace are reading reports or viewing tables of results and drawing conclusions from those data. If not done carefully, bias may be introduced at this point in many different ways. I call this final set of biases communication bias because they are all about how you present the data and make data available to others. Some of these may seem like common sense, but no matter how much they seem to make sense to you, they are very commonly made mistakes.

Transparency is important when sharing data and results with others. That means making sure that your audience should not have any question about what data are used in analysis and the language should be clear and easy to understand. If your recipient does not understand these things, they will not trust the validity or the applicability of the data results. Include citations and notes in your presentation of data so the reader knows the source of the data, which data are included, which data are excluded, and if applicable, how the data should be used. Most visualization tools provide mechanisms for including this type of information through titles, labels, legends, and text boxes. If these elements are not included, then it is up to the reader to interpret the data, and the intended message may not be received.

Duplication bias is created when the same or very similar data analyses are produced by different people or at different times or for slightly different reasons. If the same data are shown repeatedly in or the same visual treatment is applied to different sets of data, confusion could result as individuals mistake one analysis for another or one set of data that are not the data they assume are being shown. If your company has a set of standards for using a particular color palate, that may be a great place to start in creating a set of standards for data visualizations.

Location bias is a nuance that is easily overlooked. When designing visual presentations, most designers will tell you that people, at least in my culture, approach a visual by beginning in the upper left portion of the page or screen, and move left to right in a zig-zag pattern downward. We also tend to understand things beginning with the high-level more generalized information and moving to progressively more detailed information. Given this information, producing documents or visuals of data that violate these patterns may generate some confusion or bias in the interpretation of those data. There is another aspect of location that may generate some bias. If you do not have the access to data because it is not in a location that is accessible to you, you are subject to a number of biases due to missing data or data that are not understood properly.

Timing is another important consideration. Earlier we talked about the Hawthorn effect, where change the data is temporary, so evaluating some data too soon after a change will be biased because it is improved but not necessarily due to the change made to the independent variable. Timing when using data to make business decisions should also be considered carefully. The timing of the decision, and the timing associated with the data, are both subject to bias. Making a data-driven decision before you have the necessary data will potentially skew results. Making data-driven decisions using data that are no longer relevant due to time elapsed since the data were generated may lead to invalid decisions as well.

Finally, we get to the method of introducing bias that you, as a data-literate person, reading and interpreting reports and dashboards will encounter all the time. Reporting bias is introduced when data are presented in reports, particularly charts and graphs, that are either poorly designed or surreptitiously designed and do not represent the data as well as it should. There are so many ways to misrepresent data in reports that there are literally entire books on the topic. Here I will share some of the common types of mistakes and will take the topic deeper in an upcoming chapter on preparing visualizations of your own. For now, what you want to look out for are things like charts that make values in reports appear larger or smaller than they should be relative to other values. Charts should usually have a very consistent scale so that a value of 10 appears visually to be half the size of a value of 20 and a tenth the size of 100. If an axis is overly stretched or compacted, the visual can be misleading. Timelines that represent long periods of time often violate these rules. Sometimes it is acceptable as long as it is clear which part of the visual contains the data that is primary topic of the evaluation. Other methods include poor or no labeling of the axis or mixed abbreviations like mixing thousands (k) and millions (m) on a scale. It is also common for visualization designers to select a chart type that may not be appropriate for the data they are displaying or display the data in a way that is overly complex making it difficult to interpret. The more you know about how to display data, the more issues you will detect in other people's visualizations.

The goal of this chapter is to help you identify potential issues with the way data is collected, organized, evaluated, and communicated. You may, at this point, feel like it is impossible for any work with data to be perfect. You would be correct. An absolute truth does not exist. The fact that we are humans and not infallible draws everything we do into question at some level. The measure of success is not absolute, indisputable truth. If it were, none of us would ever succeed. Success in working with data is all about understanding and representing the data as best you can while avoiding as much bias as you can. If you are not purposely attempting to mislead others with data, and you do not detect any intentional bias in others' work, then we consider that very successful. Data and data-driven decision making is not a perfect science. Data can inform our decisions, but it is up to us to interpret those data and make the decisions as best we can, then validate the results of those decisions.

READING TO UNDERSTAND

Welcome to the third component of data literacy. So far, we have defined data literacy and hopefully learned a few new things about the language of data. In this section of the book, we will turn our focus to reading, interpreting, and understanding different ways data is presented in the workplace. We will begin with a discussion about the four different types of analytics and the dozen or more ways we examine data using reports and analyses. I will end this section with a tour through many different ways you may see data visualized in reports. There are new visualizations being invented every day. I will never be able to cover them all, but I hope to hit all the most common and most informative for making data-driven decisions in the workplace.

The more you learn about data literacy and how to read and communicate with data, you may even become fascinated, like I am, with how working with data involves so many different inherent capabilities that we all use constantly every day without even knowing it. There are elements of data literacy that involve psychology, learning, visual design, communications, logic, teaching, ethics, and maybe just a touch of math. Every marketing display or chart and graph, or document is laid out and organized and colored and sized with a specific message in mind, and we consume all of this without really thinking about it. Read on to learn a few tricks of the trade.

8
TYPES OF ANALYTICS

The most common way you will likely encounter data in the workplace that you are using to make data-driven decisions is through visualizations. Data visualizations on reports and dashboards are designed to provide you with results of some sort of analytics. There is a range of types of analytics, and it is helpful to know a little about each one as you absorb the information each provides. In this chapter I will discuss four main types of analytics that you are likely to encounter in the workplace. Each type of analytics provides a different value, and each is a bit more complex that the last as that value increases. I often see the four types of analytics on a chart with complexity or difficulty on the x axis (horizontal) and value on the y axis (vertical).

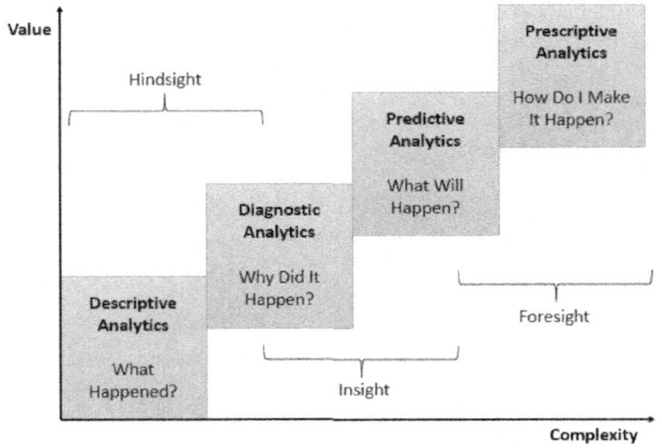

Descriptive analytics use your data to describe what is happening in your business. These analytics are usually based on live data and provide information about some aspect of your business in real-time. Reports that you typically see inside of business applications are usually describing those data that are being generated within the application through data entry or some sort of integration. Descriptive analytics are used by businesses to make data-driven decisions based on trends and patterns within their business data. It is used to track specific metrics that are important to your company and appear in company reports and dashboards either as raw data or an aggregation of many data records.

Descriptive analytics use current and historical data to look back and keep tabs on operational performance and trends. Some examples of descriptive analytics include activity tracking, sales pipeline, service request volumes, invoice data, and resolution times. Sometimes these data are presented as just a table of the data as it is recorded, and often there are some aggregations such as totals, sub-totals and averages included. Descriptive analytics data are often grouped and reported by date values or department or product line.

If you were to take a look at all of the data that your company accumulates, you would see a lot of large tables with many rows and many columns. It would be impossible to understand any trends or patterns in these raw data. With just a little bit of filtering and math, you can begin to make sense of the data. This is what descriptive analytics does for us. Some basic math and simple descriptive statistics (yes, that exists) will allow trends and patterns to emerge from vast amounts of data. If you tried to find a pattern in the number of service calls your company receives each month for several years, you would not want to attempt this by examining individual records and attempting to tally call counts in your notepad. You can use the power of descriptive analytics to create this tally for you. You have probably even developed your own descriptive analytics using a basic spreadsheet application and some totaling. And since data are everywhere, you have probably done some descriptive analytics outside of work. If you have balanced your bank account, made a packing checklist, or kept score at your kid's game, you have worked with descriptive analytics.

Even though descriptive analytics is positioned at the lower left corner of our value and complexity chart, it is extremely important to your business. Descriptive analytics are the most accessible and easiest to generate and use, so they enable everyone to understand the company's data and make well-informed data-driven decisions that benefit the company. The trends and patterns become apparent, so it is easier to see where things are going well and where some improvement is needed. It may show trends that can help you understand the seasonality of your business or which products are on an upward or downward trajectory. There are some limitations of descriptive analytics. The main shortcoming of descriptive analytics is that it is only reporting what has already happened. It cannot tell you anything about what caused the trends or patterns, or how to predict what is likely to happen next. A simple descriptive analytic report is typically only going to include two or three variables at a time.

Diagnostic analytics will take you to the next level of analysis where you are asking your data about why things happened. This is the type of analysis you perform to figure out why things happened the way they happened. Rather than asking what the results are, you ask why we received those results. Typically answering this type of question requires some more complex examination techniques. This type of analysis often involves discovery of many more datapoints, some mining of data, and an understanding of relationships, or correlations, between datapoints. If you are trying to determine why something happened using your data, and you have a hypothesis to begin with, you can select the meaningful datapoints that would expose that relationship between data that best illustrates that cause. If you are not starting with a hypothesis, then you may have to do a lot more data discovery to ensure that you are most likely to find relationships in the data that will suggest the cause.

Let's say you notice in your descriptive analytics that you seem to be selling a particular product more often now than you did before. You have a hypothesis that the change in price caused this uptick in sales. Given your hypothesis, you should gather your data on product sales and sell prices over a significant period of time. A longer period would include enough history to capture data before and since the price change. If your analysis shows that there is indeed a positive correlation between sales and price, you may be able to reasonably conclude that price is affecting sales.

Now suppose you have noticed the increase in sales, but do not have a solid hypothesis as to why sales increased. To find the possible reasons for the change, you will need to collect and examine much more data. Among other things, you collect data about the sales staff, the pricing, the service calls, competitor information, marketing data, and training data. Upon performing analysis of all these different datapoints, you may find one or more show some positive correlation.

It is important at this point to explain some things about correlation. The correlation is the statistical relationship between sets of data. A correlation value will fall between -1 and 1. A strong correlation will be closer to -1 or 1 and a lack of correlation will be close to zero. A positive correlation occurs when the value of one datapoint increases as the value of the other datapoint increases. For example, as the size of your customer increases, the number of service calls increases. If you plotted these data on a scatterplot with company size on the y axis and number of calls on the x axis, this strong positive correlation would look something like the chart below. The line among the points on the scatterplot is what the correlation value would look like if you plotted the best fit line. A line moving up and right indicates a positive correlation.

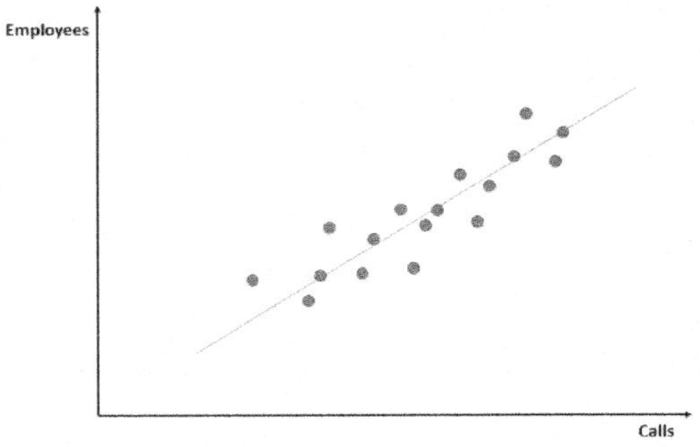

A negative correlation is not necessarily a bad thing. A correlation closer to -1 is just as strong as a correlation close to 1, it just happens to be in the other direction. Consider an example correlating sales with price. As the price increases, the number of sales decreases. This correlation line will slope downward from upper left to lower right.

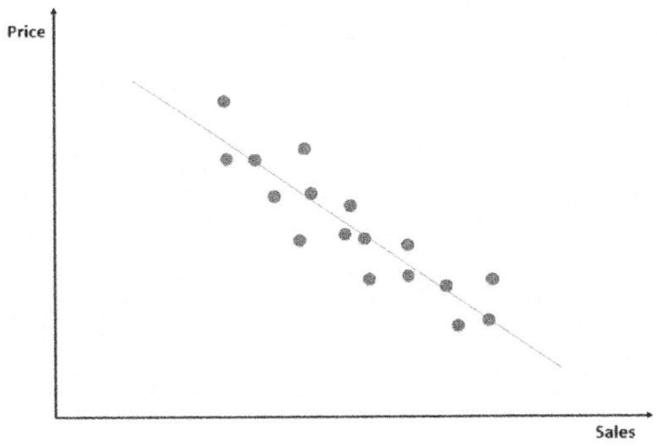

When a correlation is closer to zero indicating that it is very weak, there will be very little or no slope in the correlation line. If there is no significant correlation between price and number of service calls, there would be no obvious increase or decrease in calls as the price increases. We could rule out any possibility that the price influences the number of calls.

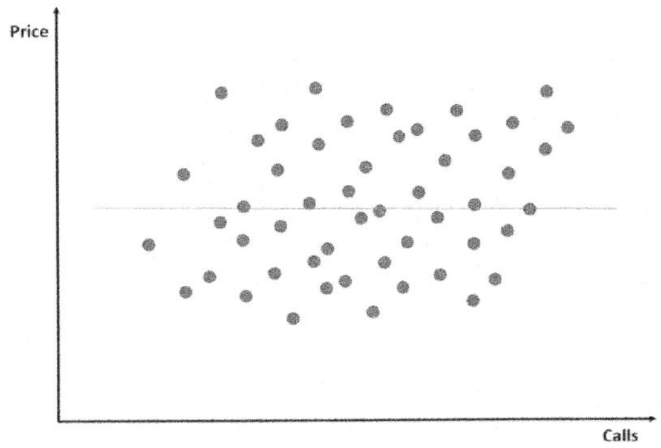

Since we are looking to answer the why question with diagnostic analytics, perhaps the most important thing to know about correlation is that a strong correlation does NOT prove causation. Two datasets can be strongly correlated and have absolutely no causal relationship. A classic example is that the sales of ice cream and the number of shark attacks have a strong positive correlation. That does not mean that increased ice cream sales are causing additional shark attacks or that ice cream sales are affected by shark attacks. What is more likely here is that when the weather is sunny and hot, people are more likely to buy ice cream and are also more likely to be swimming in the ocean where hungry sharks are hanging around. The existence of a strong correlation simply means that there is a relationship there, and that additional analysis is merited to determine if the relationship is truly a cause and effect or if there is an additional variable that could be affecting both datasets.

Diagnostic analytics are clearly a little more complex and a bit more valuable than descriptive analytics. Diagnostic analytics will enable you to get more value from your data by more deeply examining the data and asking the right questions to reach a determination of why things are happening in your business. Performing this type of analytics typically does require some more powerful analytics tools. I have done this type of analysis in a spreadsheet program, so it is possible if you are skilled with writing formulas, but newer tools make this so much easier. Imagine now how better your business decision can be made with this type of data analytics driving them.

Now we find ourselves moving from what most people call reporting and analytics or business intelligence into a new exciting realm that has come to be known by many as data science. Predictive analytics brings us out of reporting on what has already happened and analyzing for insights in the data that exists in our databases and into reporting what will probably happen in the future. With predictive analytics we use massive amounts of data, sometimes data from outside our organization, to identify relationships between various datapoints to identify leading indicators. Finding leading indicators based on trends and relationships in the data will allow us to make some predictions about what may likely happen in the future. The statistics that go into this type of analysis has been around for a long time, but modern technology is making predictive analytics more accessible than ever before.

Companies are finding predictive analytics to be very valuable and beneficial in several different ways. With predictive analytics, and the right data, it is possible to improve operations, make marketing more efficient, detect fraudulent activity, predicting which prospects will buy, which will churn, and reducing risk in many more ways. By examining historical data to see which trends are most pervasive, we can begin to discern what is likely to happen when current data matches the same trend or doesn't match that trend. If you determine that a large percentage of customers who have cancelled their service also had many complaints, you can reasonably predict that customers filing a lot of complaints are likely to cancel their service. Not exactly too difficult to guess that one without the complicated math. They are not all obvious. Suppose you do the analysis and find that when prospects of a particular industry and size are invited to a Webinar about your services and are provided testimonials from existing clients, their likelihood of buying is much greater than other scenarios. If you can expose this pattern in the data, your sales strategy for your next prospect with a similar profile is an easy decision. A data-driven decision, in fact. Banks and other lenders have used this type of analysis to determine who is most likely to default on loans. Your insurance rates are not determined randomly either.

You may have heard about "big data" in recent years. Big data are large complex data sets that are often from outside your organization. Big data can provide more variety and greater volumes in a higher velocity. In fact, there is such a volume and velocity that a typical database and basic data processing tools cannot handle it all effectively. Big data are often unstructured and require some serious computing power to make much sense of but hidden in these data are potentially valuable insights. Big data has become so popular and valuable that new technologies are being developed just to handle the massive amounts of data that are being collected by companies like Google, Facebook, Amazon, and YouTube. We are all a source of big data about our own tendencies. The more information you have about your prospects and customers, the more you can do with predictive analytics.

If you are fortunate enough to work with data scientists, you may be provided with some results of this type of analysis. They are usually in the form of a chart like a line graph that shows past performance on the left and as you more to the right, you get to and go past current date. Usually, the line goes from a solid line to a dotted line or two dotted lines that both start at the current date and continue along diverging paths, growing wider apart. I explain more about reading these types of charts later. For now, just know that a prediction is never precise, and the farther out your prediction the less precise it can be. It is not possible without some sort of paranormal abilities to make precise accurate predictions, but with enough data and the right statistical models, we can get pretty close for mortals.

Finally, the most valuable and most complex analytics are prescriptive. Prescriptive analytics not only makes predictions about the future, but it also helps make data-driven decisions by making some of those decisions for you. Prescriptive analytics answer the "what should I do next?" questions. They can allow you to do a little testing too. You can often create "what if" analyses. The methodologies used for prescriptive analytics include things like artificial intelligence, simulations, neural networks, and machine learning. Prescriptive analytics not only predicts what will happen, it predicts when it will happen and why. In this way it can suggest options on how to take advantage of future happenings or mitigate against those things that are likely to happen. Prescriptive analytics is not something that runs just once to provide a single set of results. This type of analysis relies on models that "learn" from continually incorporating new data and making new predictions based on changes in the trends and patterns within those data. This final frontier of analytics is a combination of many different disciplines such as research, natural language processing, applied statistics, and machine learning. It is as close as we can get to simulating human decision-making capabilities.

Companies are striving to move up the scale in the types of analytics being performed with their data. It is not an easy undertaking and requires a real investment in the skills and resources to get there. Data literacy is a key component in not only achieving better analytics but reaping the rewards of better analytics as well. It is far less impactful on a business to do great analytics when the workforce is unable to understand the data and make data-driven decisions using those data. Without data literacy at all levels of the organization, key information is missed or misunderstood.

9
METHODS FOR EXAMINING DATA

At this point I hope you now have a better idea of what data is and some of the things we can do with data given the right tools and enough data. There are many methods used to explore and examine data. As we review our data, there are several questions we should ask of those data to determine if we can trust the results of our explorations and gain the most value from analyses. The methods described in this chapter are not just for the data scientists or data analysts. Carefully examining data is important for anyone looking to use those data to make data-driven business decisions. Whether you are looking at raw data in a database, a table of values, or a report or dashboard showing the results of an analysis, employing these methods will help you truly understand what you are looking at. In fact, I hope this book will make you a little better at working with data regardless of where in the process you encounter those data.

The five Cs provide a good high-level framework for good data. If you have data that are complete, consistent, clean, convenient, and controlled then you are ready to question those data further and determine more about what we can learn from them. The following questions we will ask of our data will ensure that we know the data well enough to make data-driven decisions that you can trust.

1. **What is the source of these data?**
   Knowing where your data come from is very important for your confidence in those data for making decisions. If the data are from a trusted source that provides a clean and complete dataset this leads to performing analysis in which you have a high level of confidence. If you are reviewing a report or dashboard and know the source of that the data used to develop that analysis, then you are more likely to trust the results. Most companies rely on people inputting data. Employees input data into computer systems through data entry. Prospects or customers fill in online forms. There is certainly nothing wrong with collecting data in these ways, but not all data sources are trustworthy. As students we had to cite our sources on research papers. As consumers we want to know where our food comes from. Knowing the source of things gives us comfort and confidence. If we have a distrust of the source, we probably distrust the product. Why should data be any different? If you want to make data-driven decisions that others trust and you want to trust others' decisions, you need to trust the data sources used to make those decisions.
2. **Is the data live or static?**
   It is vitally important that you know if you are looking at data and making data-driven decisions based on live or static data. This is especially true if you are using a report of data from an earlier timeframe but are collecting those data from a live transactional data source. A historical report from a live data source may inaccurately reflect that history. Live data reflect the current state of

the data. If those data change, and you refresh the report or re-query those data, you will see the data as they exist in that moment, which may be different from even a moment earlier. If you are reviewing data on a report that was printed or exported last week, you need to know that those data may be different now than they were when the report was originally executed. On the other hand, if you are comparing data over a period of time according to the date those data were captured and stored in a data warehouse, you need to know that those data reflect the data as they existed at the time of that snapshot. This allows us to see how data change over time. Depending on the scope of your data need and the way the snapshots are scheduled, you can view data as they appeared at different times in the past. If the data warehouse is storing monthly snapshots, you cannot see weekly or daily changes, so it is good to know the frequency of the data capture as well.

3. **What filters have been applied to these data?**
Filters are used to refine which data are included in a dataset or used for completing the analysis. These filters typically allow you to zero in on data that are meaningful for your examination. Data that are over-filtered will not include enough data or all the relevant datapoints and may lead to poorly informed decision making. Data that are under-filtered may contain too much noise that introduces bias and confounding variables that will diminish the value of your analysis. As someone filtering the data, great care should be taken to filter data properly, which means you need to fully understand the business question you are attempting to answer with those data. As a consumer of any analyses provided for you, it is very helpful for you to also know which data are included and excluded from the analyses. Think about the different ways bias may be introduced. Selection bias is very easy to create with imprecise filtering of data.

4. **What timeframe are you working with?**
This is like the filtering question but is specifically about date ranges. You want to know that the results you are working with are from a valid timeframe. For descriptive analytics, this may be the timeframe you are describing with the data. For other analyses, you may need longer time frames to capture time-based patterns in the data. Seasonality of data is an excellent example of something that is not possible to detect with a shorter timeframe. Predicting future outcomes typically requires a massive amount of data over a long timeframe. Some special circumstances may require some specific date filters. If you want to perform a year-over-year comparison that includes the current year, you need to understand if you are comparing the same scope of data from last year to this year. If today is the middle of September, is the data from last year including all last September's data or just the data up to the middle of the month? Additionally, when questioning data involving dates and times, it is important to understand at which level (month, week, day) the data is compiled. When counting days, are we including all days of the week or only counting business days? If you are working with time, the question of time zone translation may need to be asked as well.

5. **What scale and unit of measure are you using?**
Just like working with dates and knowing if you are reporting days or months, it is vital that you understand the unit of measure for all the metrics in your data. If you are reviewing revenue reports, are the numbers reporting in thousands or millions? The units should be clearly communicated and represented appropriately on your reports in labels or chart axis lines. Are the units of measure consistent among the metrics included in the analysis? If a table of figures is presented and the columns of numbers are shown in different units, it is quite easy for someone to perform some calculations using those figures without converting the numbers to a common unit of measure. Imagine you have one column with "$1,000k" and another column with "$1,000" on the same row. If not careful, someone could easily assume a 1 to 1 ratio rather than 1,000 to 1. Unfortunately, there is no single standard and some parts of the world use the metric system and other parts use the imperial system of measurement. Both should not be used in the

same analysis if it can be avoided.

6. **Are data labels clear and descriptive?**
   Imagine opening your kitchen pantry to determine what you are going to prepare for dinner, and all the boxes and cans had lost their labels. You may be able to make some assumptions based on the type of packaging or where in the pantry items are located, but you would not really know what sort of meal you are going to make until you open things up and determine what they are. Data are like this too. If you were to look at a dataset with no column labels or an analysis with no title or axis labels, you have no idea what you are looking at and what the data are trying to tell you. You may be able to guess based on where the values are shown on a chart or the format of those values, but you do not have enough knowledge of the data to make any viable data-driven decisions. Even if the labels are there, but are not descriptive enough, you may not understand the message. Acronyms plague our business communications. As convenient as they may be, and as much space as they save on the page, they are only effective if everyone knows what the TLA stands for. Labels need to be descriptive enough for everyone to understand. Like the unit labels discussed earlier, the "k" after the number is critical to knowing the difference between 1 and 1,000. Later we will discuss some additional visual cues that can augment labeling. "TLA" by the way, stands for three letter acronyms.
7. **Are there any gaps or holes in the data?**
   Check your data for any obvious gaps or omissions. If your dataset is showing the last 10 years of information but missing a couple years in the middle, there's a chance that someone is attempting to hide some information by not including it in the data or analysis. You certainly cannot trust any trend or patterns in the data over the timespan. This is not an uncommon way some purposely introduce bias into data analyses, especially analyses that span long periods of time. It is also possible that the gaps in data are due to some over-zealous filtering which may or may not be intentional. If there are gaps, you want to be sure they are disclosed and do not impact the validity of any analyses.
8. **Is excess information included in the analysis?**
   The inverse issue of gaps in data, too much data, may not sound like a bad thing. It is not always an issue, but it can be. Excess data, if not relevant but used as if it were, can introduce bias into your analyses. Confounding variables are data that introduce bias by distracting us from the true meaning of the data or changing the results. A datapoint that is correlated with your independent variable or causally related to your dependent variable can potentially cause you to draw conclusions that will lead you astray. Data can be over-filtered or under-filtered. Under filtering data can be just as troublesome as over filtering because you may lose the focus of your data or the analysis you are reading may have too much information making it difficult to interpret.
9. **Does the data provide actionable information?**
   Can the insights made by your data be used to decide to perform a relevant action for your business? Actionable data is much more valuable than data that is merely descriptive. I am often asked to provide some sort of report that reflects data that just satisfies a curiosity. As the analyst it is not always up to me which reports I provide, and I usually have very little control over how that data is used or not used to make valid actionable decisions. What I do have control over is providing data that is clear and concise enough to tell the story so that they can be used to act. As someone who is using data to make decisions, I need to be data literate and understand those data and how the results of an analysis were derived so that I can make good data-driven decisions.
10. **Are trends in the data visible and clearly defined?**
    Something else you want to look for are trends in the data. Are values moving up or down over time? Trends in the data often lead us to deeper analyses to understand what is causing the trend or to predict what the future is likely to look like as the trend continues. A fun example of

watching trends in data is sports. If your favorite player or team has been on a hot streak, you expect that streak to continue. You make a data-driven decision to wear your team's gear out and brag about your team's record. If your team has a losing streak, you probably behave very differently. We may even do this subconsciously. When we see trends, we tend to assume that those trends will continue. Many business decisions are based on simple trends when a deeper analysis should have been conducted. Trends can be informative, and they can be misleading, but detecting a trend in the data can lead to better understanding and better decisions.

11. **Are there patterns in the data that may offer additional insight?**
Like trends, patterns in data can be super informative and help make better data-driven decisions. Let's go back to your sports team for a moment. Your team starts every season on a hot streak, but near the end of the season they begin to lose more frequently and usually end up barely keeping a winning record by the end of the season. This has happened every year for a while now. This is a pattern that may cause you to wonder why. Why does the team always start losing mid-season? This pattern has led you to the next analysis; the next question to ask your data. Patterns can be easy to spot, and sometimes nearly impossible to see. Seasonality of sales is a pattern that is usually easy to spot because it is natural to group and visualize data over time. Effectiveness of service personnel who have completed specific training programs may be difficult to see unless you are specifically looking for it. Other patterns may never be seen because they are so innocuous that you never think to look for them. That is where machine learning and artificial intelligence can become illuminating.

12. **Do sets or groups included in the analysis make sense with the purpose of the analysis?**
Grouping data allows us to see aggregate information segmented by some attribute. For instance, you may segment your sales reporting by territory or regions. You may group service data by products or type of service. The groups need to be meaningful. If you are grouping sales performance by color of the company car, does that make sense for your analysis? Perhaps it does if you have a hypothesis that people driving red cars are better salespeople. But that only makes sense if the salespeople can choose their car color and your hypothesis is that salespeople who have personalities that tend to choose red cars are more successful. I also want to caution you here on grouping data by protected classifications such as race, gender, and religion. There may very well be some trends and patterns there, but if your analysis could be used to discriminate, you probably should tread carefully. Sometimes meaningful groupings can be discovered while performing an analysis and offer a different perspective. If you notice that your data appears to be clustered into groups on a scatterplot for instance, you could isolate those data and look for commonalities that could be used to group the data in a different way.

13. **Is the purpose of the analysis obvious and meaningful?**
If you are someone who performs any sort of analysis either for yourself or others, you should always ask yourself this question. If you cannot think of any business decision you need to make or business question you need to answer, then perhaps you are wasting your time with an analysis that is not beneficial to your business. I am often asked to produce some data for someone who is just curious about things. Those requests usually fall to the bottom of my priority list. You may also know of a report or two that are produced every month or week that have been produced for years and are still being produced because that is just what has always been done. This question about the purpose of the analysis should be asked of those things as well. If they are not being used in the workplace to make data-driven decisions, are they necessary? Another way to consider this question about your analysis is to determine if the analysis is answering the business question it is intended to answer. I don't know how many times I have fulfilled a request for a report that is thousands of lines of data with dozens of columns that I know are never used for anything other than wasting paper. What possible business question is answered by a data dump into a huge table. If there is no analysis of the

data, what purpose does it serve?

If you examine your data and your visualizations of data with these questions, you will have a good idea of what those data can do for you in your workplace. Without this examination, we rely on others to interpret the meaning of data for us. If those individuals are not data literate or trained in data science, you are at the mercy of their analyses. If you are not data literate enough to question the validity of data you are provided, you will find yourself at the mercy of whatever biases are within the data along with the bias you unknowingly introduce.

Bias is a fascinating topic related to data science. You want to avoid biasing your data as much as possibly, but eliminating bias entirely is neither possible nor is it desirable. I know it sounds as if I am contradicting myself here, but bias will always exist in the analysis of data because you have innate biases that you cannot turn off that may impact how you interpret data. Without writing a thesis here on chaos theory and psychological bias, it is difficult to explain the contradiction. Making a decision requires some level of bias because you are choosing one thing over another for some reason, and you chose to ask a question of the data for a reason. But removing the human factor from data analysis and decision making will not remove the bias. When we perform data mining looking for correlations, we are identifying groups and patterns and trends using all that we know in the data, and those findings affect our decisions. Technically this is also bias because you are selecting the data that supports a decision and effectively making more decisions based on the results of that decision.

Have you ever met a child that always asks "Why?" after every statement made to them? This is annoying, but it illustrates that any fact or decision can be questioned. The statement that "there is no such thing as an absolute truth" is contradictory of itself because if there is no such thing as an absolute truth, the fact that there is no absolute truth cannot be absolutely true either. Our goal in data literacy in the workplace should not be to seek any absolute truth, but to identify the best truth given the data at our disposal. If you can determine the next best action, perform that action, and collect data on how effective that action was, you now have more data to inform the question to determine if that action was indeed the best one.

We must accept that biases exist, that no dataset is truly complete, and that the answers we get from our data are not necessarily the answers we will get when we add more data. Data literacy can help us make fewer mistakes perhaps, but it also allows us to learn more from those mistakes and successes so we can continue to make fewer mistakes and be more successful.

10
INTRODUCTION TO DESCRIPTIVE STATISTICS

You may be relieved to know that this book's intention is to help you improve your data literacy, it is not meant to turn you into a data scientist, or even a data analyst. The name of this chapter may sound like a college class that you would not want to take but will not be that painful. I personally enjoyed my statistics classes, but if you did not or have not ever taken one, I will give you just enough information in this chapter to sound like you did. You might even better understand what the math nerds like me are saying or showing you in their data visualizations.

Fact is, you do need to understand a few things about descriptive statistics to be data literate. You do not need to be able to read the equations or solve any formulas to be data literate, but you do need to know what some of these things mean. This chapter will present a dozen or so concepts that will cover 99% of the mathematical principles you will encounter in the workplace. Okay, I made up that statistic. That just illustrates why it is so important for you to know a little bit about how this works. People make up statistics all the time, and people believe those made-up statistics a lot the times. Just because you see something in print, you should not assume that it is accurate or unbiased or not completely made up.

Descriptive statistics is a field of mathematics that is used to describe qualitative and quantitative data. Statistics are used to understand how data behave by examining those data and how each datum relates to the others. This concept is not foreign to you, because we all do this naturally when we make generalizations about things, we encounter every day. How do you know what time to leave the house each day to arrive at work on time? You use concepts present withing descriptive statistics without all the complicated math. If I asked you how long your drive to work typically takes, you could give me that answer easily. You might even say something like "on average, it takes…" when answering. But what about that one time when it took three times longer because you blew a tire and had to wait for roadside assistance? You wouldn't factor that into your average commute time. That's called an outlier. If I asked you the quickest you have ever made the commute and the longest time it has taken, you can probably give me that range of data as well. What if I asked you why you leave earlier on a Monday than you do on a Friday? Do you think you could explain that you can usually get to work quicker on Fridays because more people take that day off and traffic is usually a bit lighter? That sounds oddly like correlation and probability to me. You are a statistician, like it or not.

Let's start with the average time it takes for you to get to work. That calculation is also called the "mean" value. You are already familiar with the concept of average, and you may even know how to calculate it by totaling all the values and then dividing by the total number of values. Of course, even this simplest of concepts – divide the total value by the number of values looks intimidating when you are shown what the statistical formula looks like for the mean value of a list of values. I don't want this to be

$$\frac{1}{n}\sum_{i=1}^{n} x^{i}$$

intimidating, so I am going to discuss these measures without focusing on all the math involved.

There is a problem with the mean value. It is affected by outliers. Outliers are extreme values that are outside the normal. They do not fit the pattern for all the other data values. Let's take that drive to work. If you record your drive times for a month, and they all are between 30 and 40 minutes, you might say that the average or mean commute time is around 35 minutes. If at one point during that month, it took you 90 minutes to get to work, you would still say your normal mean commute is 35 minutes, not 50 minutes because of the one anomaly. That is because you are naturally removing the outlier. Of course, if you are truly calculating the mean commute time, mathematically your mean is greater than 35 because the mean uses all the data in the calculation. This example helps us understand the value of the median.

Median means middle. If you arranged the twenty-one commute times you recorded for a month in order from shortest to longest, and then found the 11th value in the list. That is the median value. It is probably somewhere around 35 minutes. The fact that there is a value in the list that is very much outside the norm does not affect the median. If you kicked that anomalous values out of the list, the median will still be around 35 minutes. Because median is not susceptible to the effects of an outlier in the data, it is often a more desirable measure of central tendency. I believe as a society we have put too much focus on mean and not enough on median. The comparison to the mean seems to be pervasive. Everyone wants to be above average, which of course is impossible, but I have never been told that my goal should be to be above the median, but that's really what we are trying to do, isn't it? The goal is to have a winning record, be in the top half.

To find the median, you must determine the range of the data. In other words, you need to find the lowest value (minimum) and the highest value (maximum) and if you were to calculate the difference between minimum and maximum, you have the range. If the fastest commute for you has been 25 minutes and the longest was 90 because of that flat tire, your minimum is 25 minutes and your maximum is 90 minutes, making the range 65 minutes. There are 65 minutes between 25 minutes and 90 minutes. Now we know the lowest value is 25 minutes, the median value is 35 minutes, and the maximum value is 90 minutes. We can also segment this data into quartiles.

Quartiles are like the median, which splits the list of values into two halves, only with quartiles, we are dividing the list into four parts. This will be an important concept to understand when examining data in a box and whisker chart for instance. By identifying the range of each quartile, we can begin to understand how the values are spread out along a scale. We can get an idea of where on the scale we will see most of the values. Let's go back to our commute time example and identify some key points.

Here is our data. They have been arranged in ascending order.

25, 29, 30, 30, 31, 32, 32, 33, 34, 35, 35, 35, 36, 36, 37, 37, 38, 39, 39, 40, 90

First, we will find the median, which is the middle number in the set.

25, 29, 30, 30, 31, 32, 32, 33, 34, 35, **35**, 35, 36, 36, 37, 37, 38, 39, 39, 40, 90

Now we find the median of the lower and upper halves of the dataset. We do not include the median, so we have two sets of 10 values each. To get a median when the number of values is even, we take the average of the two middle numbers.

25, 29, 30, 30, 31, 32, 32, 33, 34, 35

Median of this set is 31.5; the average of 31 and 32. We will call this Q1

35 (Median) We will call the median of the entire set Q2

35, 36, 36, 37, 37, 38, 39, 39, 40, 90

Median of this set is 37.5; the average of 37 and 38 which we will call Q3

Now we can identify five important places on our scale. The minimum, maximum, Q1, Q2, and Q3.

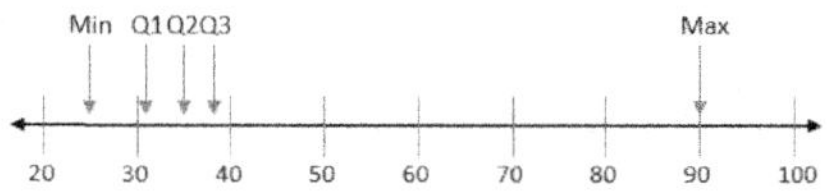

The First quartile is from Min to Q1. The second quartile is from Q1 to the median Q2. The third quartile is from Q2 to Q3, and finally the fourth quartile is from Q3 to our Max.

Roughly the same number of values exist within each quartile. The bigger the range between the first and last values in each quartile is the range for that quartile. Notice that the range of the first three is very small compared to the range of the fourth quartile. This is because we have the presence of an outlier in our dataset. That one terrible day when it took 90 minutes to get to work is skewing the data and making it more difficult to understand wholistically.

An outlier is a datapoint or datum that is statistically very different from the rest of the data. It is either an extreme high or an extreme low that exists due to some variability in the measurement or error. Since that 90-minute commute included a flat tire and this is not a normal part of our commute, we can consider it an outlier and treat it separately. When we do that, Q3 becomes 37 and Max becomes 40 and our data becomes easier to evaluate.

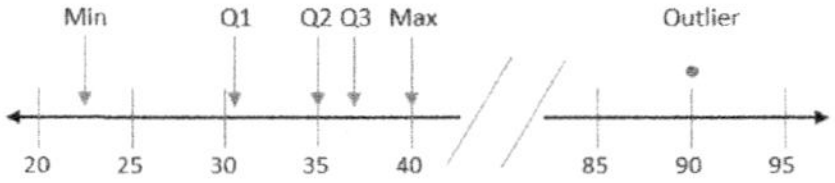

Now it is much easier to compare the ranges of the quartiles and we can see that we can occasionally get to work in less than 30 minutes, but that three quarters of the time, we should expect a commute of at least 31 minutes, but be prepared for it to take between 37 and 40 minutes a quarter of the time. You will see this structure again in the box and whisker plot, which I hope will make much more sense to you now that you realize you have been doing statistics in your head all this time.

So far, we have discussed measures of central tendency. This is what the phenomenon is called that somehow, the larger the dataset the closer it gets to fitting a distribution curve where most of the data appears in the center of the range. When communicating with others, try to avoid words like "normally" or "usually" or "typically" or "most often" when describing these measurements. It is important to be clear and distinguish between an average (mean) and a median.

There are a couple of other concepts I want to mention here before we get into more of the predictive statistics. Behavior of the data is often described using calculations of variance and standard deviation. These are not terms that are used widely in the workplace, but the statistics those terms describe most certainly are, so let us make sure you are familiar with them at least at a high level.

Variance is a measurement of how dispersed data are. A dataset with a large variance will be spread out over a larger range. By measuring the distance from the mean of each value, we can begin to assess things like risk and probabilities. Investors rely on variance when evaluating stock purchases for instance. To determine the variance of our commute time data, you would find the average of the data, which I will round to 37 for simplicity, then you would determine the difference from the mean for each value. You would then have a set of numbers ranging from -12 to 53. We want to only work with positive numbers because distance from one point to another does is not positive in one direction and negative in the other. You do not drive 40 miles from your house to the office and -40 miles back home. Without going into the math any further here, I will just explain that the negative values are eliminated, then the average of those numbers give us the variance. Our commute sample data has a variance of 162.86. If we remove our outlier, the variance of the data is only 15. The larger the variance value, the more dispersed the data is, and that is really what you need to know. If during your workday you hear that there is a large variance in the data, you will know that means the data values are very dispersed over a large range.

You may also hear about standard deviation. Standard deviation is also a measurement of dispersion relative to the mean. Just like variance, if the standard deviation is higher, then so is the amount of dispersion. Maybe it is enough for you to know that standard deviation as a calculation is just the square root of the

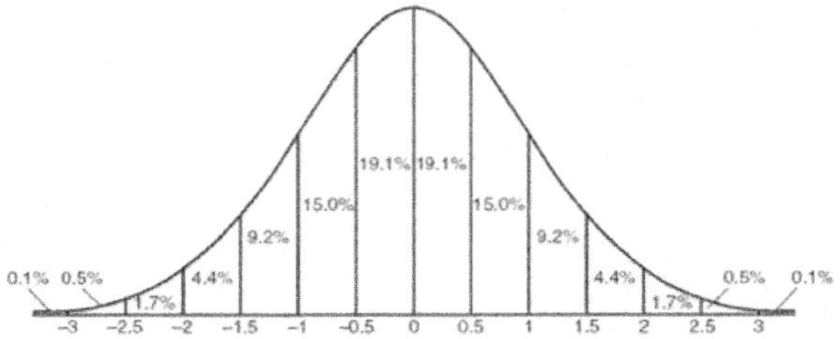

variance, but there is another special use for standard deviation that you may find interesting. We can make inferences about data using standard deviation to estimate how much of the data is within specific ranges. You will see this chart again in the next chapter, so for now, look at the percentages in each section of the curve, which plots the number of values. The percentages are a standard used to estimate how much of the data is near the mean, within a few standard deviations. The standard deviation of our commute data is approximately 13. That is the square root of our variance (162.86) with a little rounding for simplicity. Our mean is approximately 37 so one standard deviation from the mean is 24 on the low side and 50 on the high side. That indicates that according to our sample approximately 68% of our commute times will be between 24 and 50 minutes. Our outlier is truly an anomaly at over four standard deviations from the mean. A 90-minute commute is not supposed to happen.

If we were to plot this on a chart like the one above, it would show a positive skewness. Skewness is a distortion in the symmetry of the bell curve. When everything is perfect with zero skewness, the median and mean are at the center of the curve in what is called a normal distribution. Very few things are ever perfectly normal. There is always some skewness in the data. Even without doing the math or drawing the curves on a chart, you can determine if data is skewed positively or negatively by comparing the mean and the median. If your mean is greater than your median, then you have positive skew. More of the data values will be on the lower half of the range. If your mean is less than your median, then you have a negative skew. More of the data are in the second half of the range. Skewness can also indicate the direction of your outliers. If you have large value outliers in your data, the skew is positive. Low value outliers are indicated by a negative skew. This becomes important when thinking about how to predict behavior. If you have a positive skew, it is more likely that future data will also fit this pattern and be on the lower side of the range. Data scientists and analysts will consider things like skewness when training prediction models.

Another concept that you need to be familiar with as a data literate worker is correlation. So far, we have examined how datapoints are related to the mean, or how far from center they are. Correlation also measures a relationship between datapoints, but this measure is how two datapoints and the movement of those data are related. When values rise in one variable, do values in the other variable also rise or do they fall? The correlation between sales and profit for instance. If we were to plot sales price and profit, which direction does the data move? Probably there would be a positive correlation because as sales price increases, so does profit in a normal scenario. The correlation coefficient is a value between -1 and 1 where 0 indicates no relationship at all. A negative correlation is one where one variable value decreases as the other increases. Any correlational coefficient near -1 or 1 indicates the presence of a strong correlation. A positive correlation would be closer to 1 and would be seen in data where one variable increases as the other variable increases. The amount of math involved to calculate the correlation is scary to most, but software makes it very accessible now.

Understanding how different related variables behave is the key to making predictions and data-driven decisions. If data analysis has shown you that an action seems to have a relationship with a positive result, then it makes sense to keep doing that action. Correlation alone is not enough to prove causation. Proving causation requires a much more thorough investigation of the data and repeated testing. Causation may be inferred but take care if making any claims about proof of causation.

Speaking of making predictions, have you ever answered someone's question using the word "probably"? We all do this in some form or another, but as humans we can predict probabilities in our heads without ever understanding the math involved in calculating actual probability. Probability is a number between 0 and 1 (or 0% and 100%) where 0 would indicate impossibility and 1 would indicate absolute certainty. To calculate probability, you just divide the total number of times something is going to happen by the total number of possible outcomes. You do this all the time when you are making decisions. I imagine that you decide to do things or not do things based on your estimation of the probability for success. Of course, there is very real math behind calculating probabilities with data.

If you were to flip a coin, that is one action that has two possible outcomes. The probability of seeing heads is 0.5 and the probability of seeing tails is 0.5. The probability of rolling a six-sided die and getting the 6 on the top side of the die is 1 divided by 6 or roughly 0.167. If you were to roll two dice, the probability of getting 6 on both dice is 1 divided by the 36 possible combinations from rolling two 6-sided dice or 0.0278 (2.78%). Probability calculations can get rather complex, and I am not going to try to explain all the possible variations and theories around probability. In the workplace you may encounter probability calculations in things like forecast reports and predictive analytics, so it is important that you understand that probability is affected by the number of times something is performed and the number of possible outcomes. There may be other factors involved like other independent variables that affect the outcome. There are many different actions that may need to be accounted for and even more possible outcomes. The math involved is not terribly complex, but there are many different things that affect how you would calculate probability in events more complex than coins and dice. Things like disjointed events, independent events, and conditional events affect the way probability is calculated.

Hopefully you are a little less intimidated by statistics if you began just chapter with some trepidation. If you just discovered a passion for statistics, I encourage you to dig deeper and learn more. It is a fascinating discipline, but if your goal is to simply improve your data literacy, please take this bit of statistical knowledge with you as you read on and learn about how these statistics show up on your reports and dashboards.

11
DATA VISUALIZED

Earlier I mentioned that a data dump into a table with hundreds of rows and dozens of columns is useless in the workplace. No valid decisions are likely to be made by looking at data in this way. Data needs to be visualized in some way to provide meaningful answers to business questions. Data literacy is a critical skill when it comes to both creating data visualizations and reading data visualizations in the workplace. In this chapter, I will share with you how to read data visualizations. Later in the book, I will offer some tips on creating visualizations of your own.

Visualizations come in all sorts of styles from the simplest to extremely complex, but they all have one thing in common. They are meant to convey a message about the data. Sometimes that message is an explicit answer to a question, and other times the message is meant to help you arrive at an answer and perhaps ask another question. Within this chapter we will look at many different styles of charts and data visualizations and how you can read them to understand the data they show. Additionally, we will look at some additional indicators that may appear on charts to help you understand something more about the data.

Single Metric

73%

Cases Resolved Same Day

Perhaps the simplest of all, the single metric chart provides the results of a single calculation performed within the analysis. You will often find these on dashboards with multiple visualizations of different datapoints. Usually, the description of the calculation will appear either above or below the value, which is displayed in a large font on the visualization.

Table

Tables display data values in columns and rows. The intersection of the column and row contains a value described by the row and column labels. In this sample, the East region has $209,000 in their pipeline. The data in this table is aggregated and grouped by region which is the leftmost column. Tables often include subtotal and total rows that show the aggregated value for the column section or entire column. Some tables will include a column that shows an aggregation for each row across columns.

Region	YTD Sales	Pipeline Value	Deals in Pipe
North	$32,500	$112,800	14
South	$49,000	$305,000	19
East	$28,750	$290,000	16
West	$45,000	$98,000	10
Total	$155,250	$805,800	59

Pivot Table / Crosstab

	Sales				
Region	Q1	Q2	Q3	Q4	YTD Sales
North	$9,000	$13,500	$10,000	$0	$32,500
South	$12,000	$13,000	$24,000	$0	$49,000
East	$4,500	$13,250	$11,000	$0	$28,750
West	$10,500	$13,500	$21,000	$0	$45,000
Total	$36,000	$53,250	$66,000	$0	$155,250

A pivot table or crosstab is like a table but typically has the same metric split across multiple columns. You read a pivot table the same way you would a table, but with a pivot table, the data may be grouped by multiple attributes such as in this example where data is grouped by Region and Quarter. Totals may appear across the columns and across the rows. Some pivot tables include some additional interactivity that you can use to adjust the groupings or swap the metrics or break the table into sections and pages.

Pie Chart / Circular Area

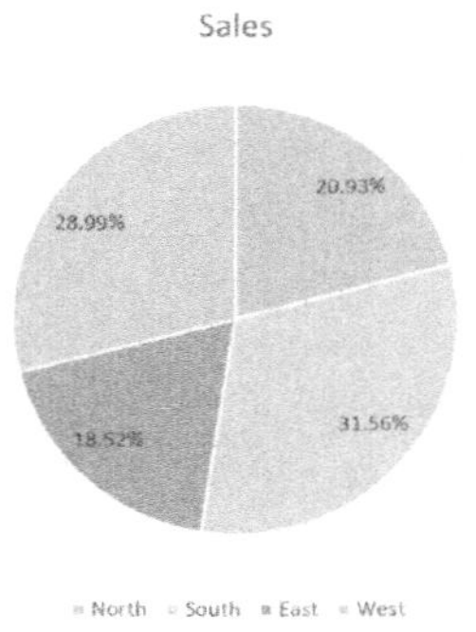

The pie chart is my least favorite of all visualizations. This is mainly because they are so often used in such a way that the data presented is unclear or is not the type of data that should appear in a pie chart. The entire circle should represent 100% of something. Let's say we are charting % of Sales Volume for our company. Each wedge in the chart represents one variable that we are using to group the data such as region. The size of the wedge is equivalent to the portion of the 100% represented by that group. I will discuss some common mistakes people make when creating pie charts in the next section of the book. Assuming you are reading a pie chart that is used appropriately, it should be easy to understand exactly how much of the data is represented by each piece of the pie.

Donut Chart

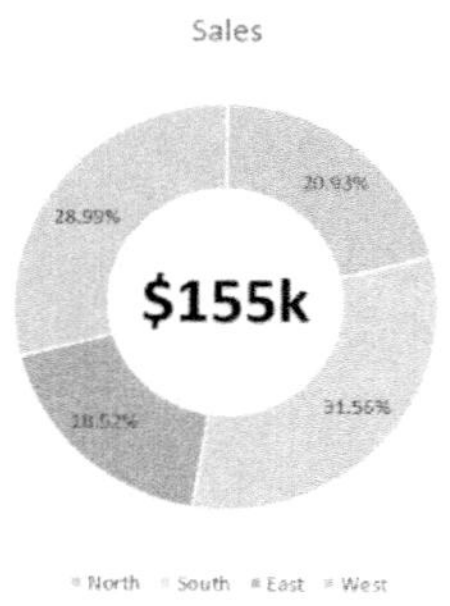

The donut chart is basically a pie chart with a hole in the center. Often that hole will contain a single metric visualization within in. The length of the arc that forms each part of the donut is sized according to the percentage of the whole that is represented. The metric in the center, if included, can be a related value such as the entire total of the values that make up the whole donut chart. You may also see the donut chart used with only two values, with one of those values displayed without color so that it appears to just be a single arc that will complete the circle if it gets to 100%. This is using a donut chart more like a gauge.

Area Chart

An area chart contains two variables, each shown on an axis. In this example we have dates along the *x* axis, which is the horizontal that is typically along the bottom of the chart. On the *y* axis we have a scale showing the number of products shipped. The y axis is vertical and typically located on the left side of the chart. The shaded portion of the chart represents the data values. Area charts are effective at showing how cumulative values change over time. Ideally data labels will be included to make it easy to see the values represented. When reading any chart that has the *x* and *y* axis included in the visualization, always pay special attention to the value where the *x* and *y* axis meet. If the value on the *y* axis is not zero at this intersection, examine the chart carefully so you can understand what may be missing from the data.

Stacked Area

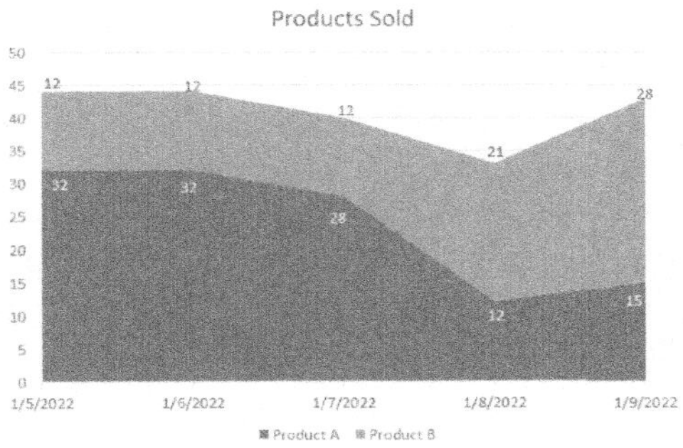

A stacked area chart is an area chart with two or more dimension values stacked up as you see in the example here. The combination of both areas represents the sum of each product on each date. This allows you to visually see the differences between the values for each data by comparing their size. It is important to have the data labels visible on this type of chart otherwise you will find yourself having to do some mental math to calculate the value of the upper areas since the *y* axis scale will only give you information about the total. If this chart did not have labels, you would have to guess that Product B sold approximately 44 minus 32 units to gather than 12 units sold.

Filled Area

A filled area chart is an area chart that shows the percentage of a total made up by each series. In this example we see the same data as the stacked area chart above, but rather than showing the specific counts, it is showing the percentage of the total represented by each value. This is like a pie chart but allows for multiple values for the time variable. Ideally this chart would include data labels that would provide either the specific counts or the percentages or both for each datapoint.

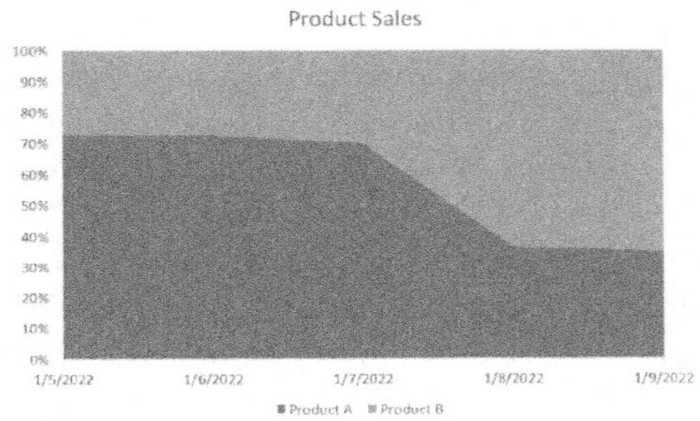

Column/Bar Chart

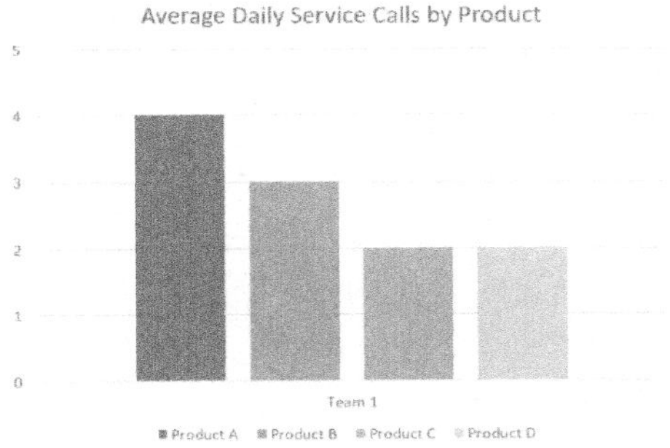

The column or bar chart is probably the chart most people are familiar with. This chart shows a value on the *y* axis and a bar for each dimension value measured. The sample chart here is showing the average number of daily service calls broken down by product for Team 1. In this chart, the data is simple enough to understand without added data labels and the legend helps us identify the product that each bar represents. In addition to the specific values for each bar, placing these bars side-by-side allows a visual comparison across products, so it is quite easy to see which product has the highest average daily service call total.

Grouped Column/Bar

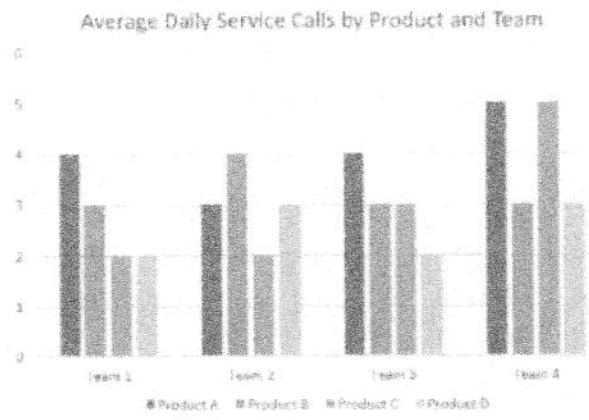

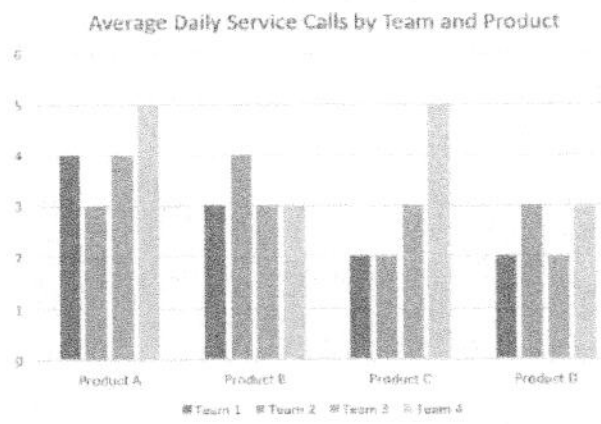

The grouped column/bar chart allows for another dimension by drawing a column chart for each value of the added dimension. In the chart above we only showed one team. If we wanted to reproduce that same analysis with multiple teams, a grouped chart gives us that flexibility. This chart is read just like the normal column/bar chart but with this grouped chart, you can not only visualize a comparison between products, but you can also compare the charts for each team. This first version provides bars for each product, grouped by team. This is appropriate if your business question is "on average, how many service calls for each product does each team handle per day?" Suppose the question is "on average, how many service calls does each team handle for each product per day?" The difference on those two business questions is almost indiscernible. In situations like this, context becomes very important. If you are a manager of one of the teams, the first chart is likely more important to you, but if you are a product manager the second chart might be what you are looking for.

Stacked Column/Bar

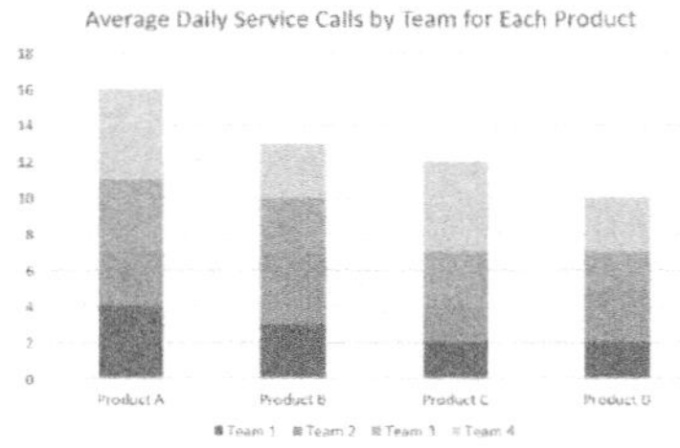

Another way to visualize the same data used in the grouped bar chart is seen in the stacked bar. In a stacked bar, each group value has a single bar, but it is segmented into stacked pieces with each piece representing a different variable. This is useful if you want to see a total for each product and want to visually see a comparison between the teams for each product. The drawback here is that the individual values are more difficult to see, and in this case the total for each team across products is difficult to determine.

Histogram

A histogram is technically a bar chart, but it shows a count of records that fall into ranges of values. Test scores are commonly shown in histograms. Histograms may be used in the workplace sometimes as well. Satisfaction survey scores or credit scores are a couple of examples. In the histogram here, we have a dataset of values between 1 and 25. We want to display the frequency of scores, but rather than showing a count of each value from 1 to 25, the values are grouped into bins. Each bin contains a range of scores, and each bar shows the number of records within each bin. In the example, we have split our range of values into 6 bins with a width of approximately 4. We can see here that most of the values fall between 9 and 17, with about a quarter of the records having a value below 9 and a quarter of records above 17. Usually, histograms are used to visualize very large datasets, and very large datasets when plotted on a frequency histogram often take the shape of a bell. This is known as the normal bell curve and if you ever decide to learn more about statistics, you will encounter this type of analysis often.

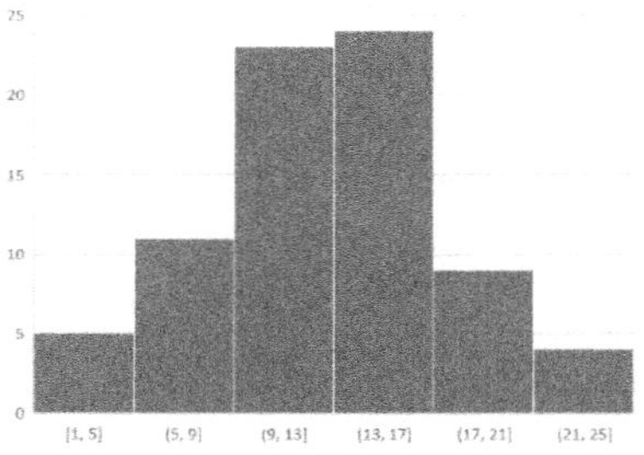

Density Curve (Function Plots)

A density curve is like a histogram but is in the form of a line chart. When we want to know about how data is distributed those data can be visualized over continuous intervals or time periods. Using a statistical smoothing algorithm called kernel smoothing the line is made into a smooth curve where the highest point(s) in the curve represent the interval most represented in the data. The chart is showing the distribution of data from a point. If you were plotting call time distribution, you might use a timeline of minutes beginning with 0 and progressing through to the minutes of the longest call. The distribution of call times will likely form a curve that will peak at the most common call times. This will provide you with a shape of a distribution. You can visually see what the most common call time is and depending on the shape of the distribution you can tell if it is more common for call times to be shorter or longer.

The density curve is also very important to statistics, particularly around the topic of standard deviation. The standard deviation is a measure of the amount of variation of a set of values from the mean (average) of those values. If something is within one standard deviation from a value, it is part of approximately 70% of the data. Data scientists will often use a measure of standard deviation to identify outliers – datapoints that are several standard deviations from the mean. When we normalize a curve, we are measuring the distribution of data from the mean. The peak of the curve is the average and is 0 standard deviations. In a normal distribution, the line takes the shape of a bell. The area

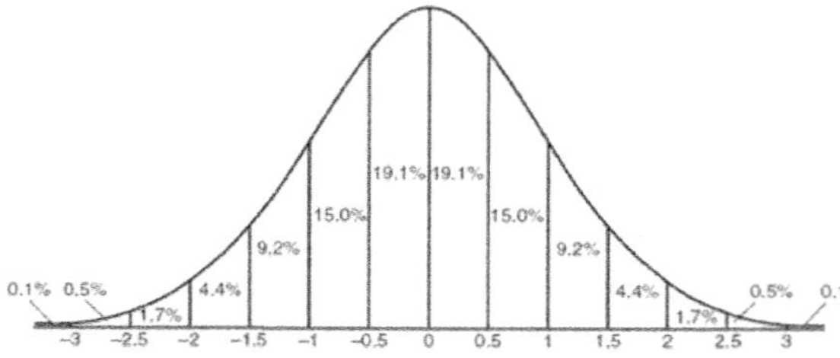

below the curve represents the density of the data at that distance from the mean. 68.2% of the data is within one standard deviation below or above the mean. 95.4% of the data is within two standard deviations.

Horizontal Bar

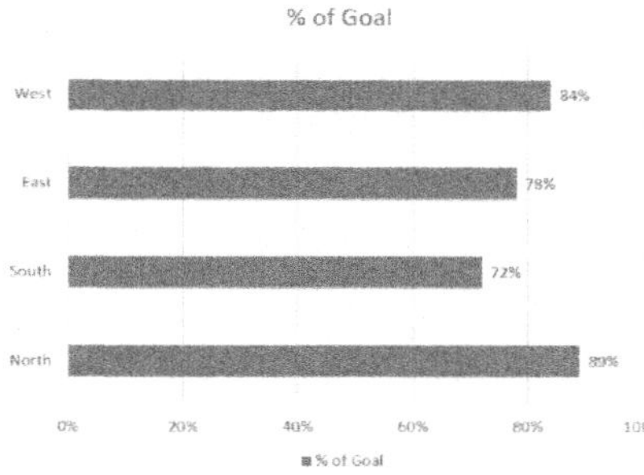

The horizontal bar chart is essentially a column bar chart turned on its side. This chart shows a value on the x axis and a horizontal bar for each dimension value measured. In the sample chart you can see the progress toward a goal for each region. I like to use the horizontal bar char for metrics that show progress or time. As humans, we tend to perceive time in a left to right orientation and totals in a vertical orientation. You can imagine this chart to be like a snapshot from a race where it is obvious that North is in the lead and South is in last so far. The added data labels and the legend helps us identify the subject of the chart and the specific value that each bar represents.

Stacked Horizontal Bar

Like their vertical counterparts, the horizontal bar chart can be stacked or grouped to allow for another dimension. In the stacked horizontal bar, each region value has a single bar, but it is segmented into stacked pieces with each piece representing a different product. The word "stacked" seems like the wrong descriptor for this chart. When I think of stacking, it is usually not side-by-side. This sideways stacking is useful if you want to see a total for each region and want to visually see a comparison between the products for each region.

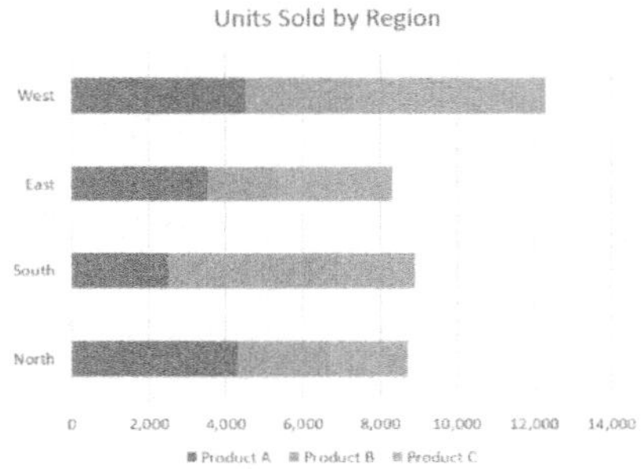

Grouped Horizontal Bar

This chart is read just like the normal horizontal bar chart but with this grouped chart, you can not only visualize a comparison between products, but you can also compare the charts for each region. This version provides bars for each product, grouped by region. Whether you use the vertical or horizontal bars, is just a matter of personal preference. You may also select based on the space you are wanting to fill with the chart. Often in the workplace we are viewing data on a screen, which is wider than it is tall, so the horizontal bar often fits better. If the chart is printed on paper, a vertical bar may fit the space better. In the end, if you can read and understand the data being presented, then either layout is acceptable.

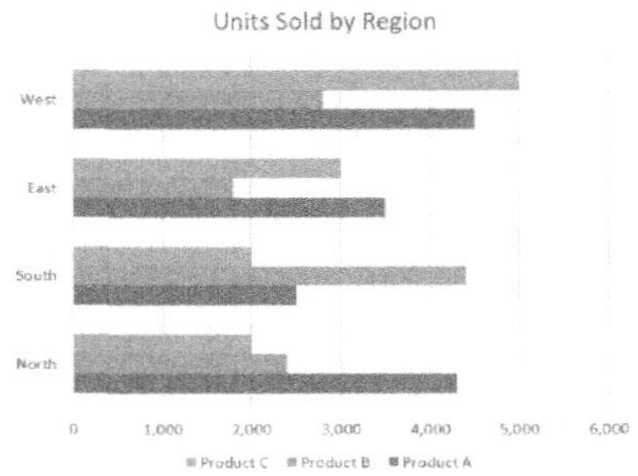

Dot Plot

A dot plot is like a vertical column chart, but rather than showing the data in solid columns, a stack of dots shows the count for each value. Suppose you were to survey the staff on how many times each week they take their lunch at their desk rather than leaving or going to the break room. If you plot your results on a dot plot, it may look something like the chart on the right. This type of chart works well with small numbers. You may also see a similar dot plot that only plots the totals. Usually if a dot plot is only showing the total, it will include a vertical axis or data labels so you can discern the value of each dot.

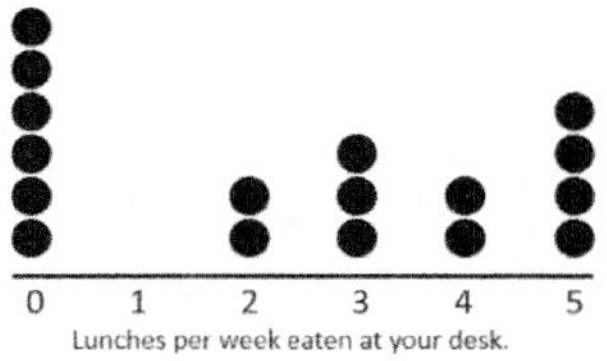

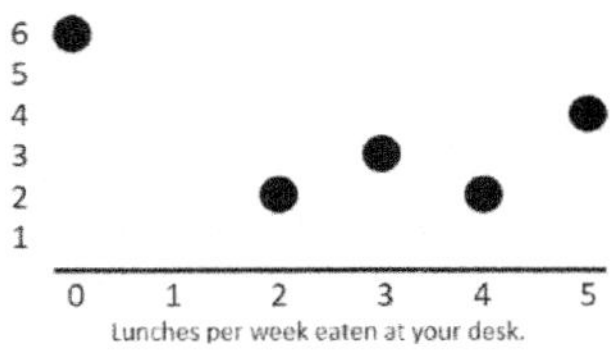

Waterfall

Waterfall charts are used for several different types of analyses where a running total is a metric of interest.

Areas like staffing, inventory, and performance are commonly visualized on a waterfall chart. The waterfall chart separates the increases and decreases so it is easy to visualize the data moving in both directions. Take this staffing waterfall chart for example. The increases and decreases in staff are visible rather than a single net number for each quarter. For Q1 you see that 23 were added and 12 were lost which tells us something about the movement of the data more so that a single Q1 measure of 11 additional salespeople. This example shows multiple additions and multiple losses over time with a total included mid-year. Some waterfall charts are less concerned with time and just show a beginning total one bar for positive and one bar for negative and then a current total. Waterfalls are also useful for visualizing profit by beginning with recommended sale price and showing the amount of discounts applied, the amount paid out in commissions, and amount spent on production to arrive at the total profit. This type of visualization makes it easy to see what is eating into profits.

Bullet

Invented by Stephen Few, the bullet chart is the newest chart style in this book and has quickly become a favorite of mine for the

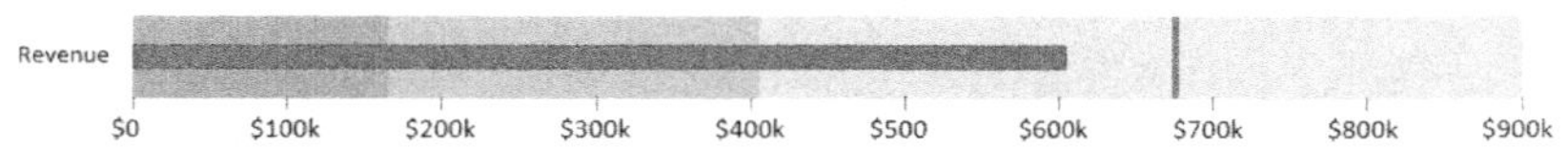

wealth of information that can be packed into the chart without using up a lot of real estate on my visualizations or dashboards. The bullet chart consists of a background gauge of sorts with shaded areas representing a qualitative range. The dark line in the foreground provides the measurement. The vertical line on the chart shows a target or goal. The axis displays the values, and additional data labels may be included to show the actual value of the bar, the target value, and to define the qualitative ranges shaded in the background.

Line

The line chart is a classic. It is usually very easy to understand and is most often used to show values over time or some other progression. The *x* axis provides the qualitative values and the *y* axis the quantitative scale for the metric visualized on the line. Each point along the line is sometimes shown with a marker and the position of that point reflects the value of the measure you are examining. In this sample, we are looking at a small profit chart in millions of dollars over a 4-year span. It is very easy to see which years were up or down from previous years.

Multi-line

Line charts may also be used to compare values. Suppose you wanted to show a line chart like the one above by region. You would have a multi-line chart like this one with a separate line for each region. It is also possible that you will encounter a multi-line chart that is showing multiple measurements. This can be misleading if all the measurements do not fit along the same scale. You may also see charts with a second vertical axis on the right side of the chart. In cases like this, if the scales

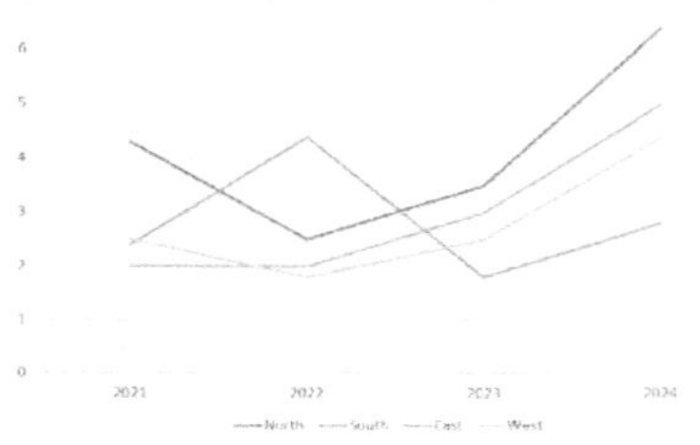

are not synchronized, two lines at the same point on the chart will represent different values. This is not a recommended approach, but I have seen it used in cases where the visualization was intended to mislead.

Dual Axis (Line Bar)

The Dual Axis, or Line Bar chart displays some data in column bar chart format and additional data as a line atop that bar chart. This type of chart may have more than one vertical axis unless the data being measured are the same datapoint as in this example. Here I only need the one vertical axis because all the datapoints described on this chart are counts of service calls. The bars represent the number of service calls of each product taken by each team. The line represents the number of service calls resolved on the same day as the call was received, also by each team, but not distinguishing between products. Personally, I prefer line bar charts that are like this, with a single axis unless the measurement formats are completely different. If one axis is counts and the other percentages like in the pareto chart below, and the context is clear, then I find that acceptable. Otherwise, multiple vertical axis scales become confusing or misleading.

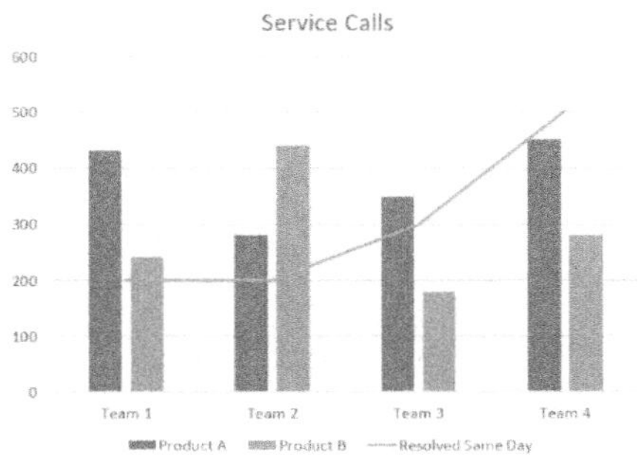

Pareto

A pareto chart is a special line bar chart that shows frequency by category on the bars with a running percent of total on the line. The left axis shows the count. The categories are sorted from largest to smallest. This allows you to easily see which category is the most significant. The right axis shows the scale for percent of total from 0% to 100%. Visually, if the line is moving higher on the chart very steeply, you will notice that you have significantly larger numbers in the most frequent categories. If the line appears closer to a 45-degree angle, the values of the bars will be more consistent. In the sample here it is easy to see that login issues are the most common and represent the largest number of cases. Bugs in the software are the least common.

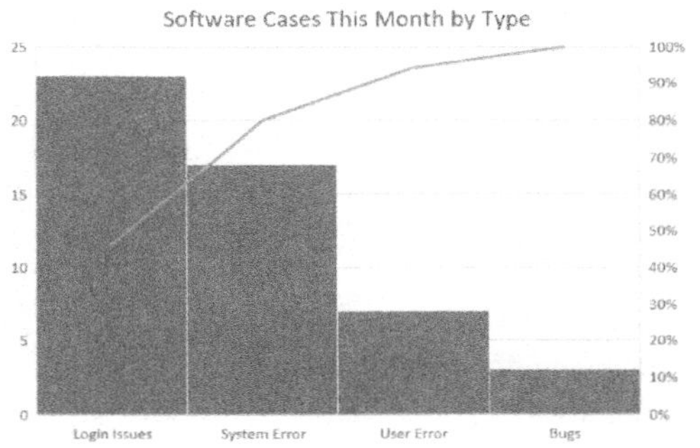

Radar (Spider)

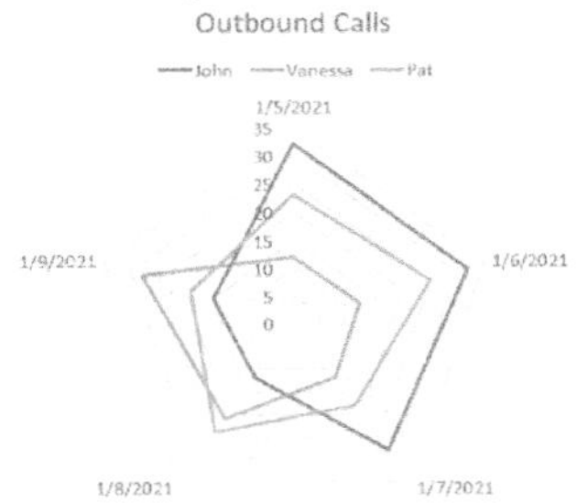

If you can imagine taking a multi-line chart and bending it around so that the end of the chart connects back to with the beginning of the chart, you might come up with something that looks like this chart. This is the radar chart or spider chart. It provides an interesting visual. In this case it is a pentagram with five points, but it could have more. Fewer than 5 does not work very well, visually. With this type of chart, it is easy to see which value is the largest and smallest at each point. It is not quite as simple to determine the values of those points along each line. A variation of this chart is a filled radar, which you may find takes a little more effort to read.

Scatter Plot

A scatter plot is a chart that uses cartesian coordinates to place markers that represent the intersection of the *x* coordinates and *y* coordinates. This type of chart is great for showing the relationships between two variables. Suppose you want to see if there is a relationship or pattern in the data for customers between the number of units purchased and the number of service claims made. Such a plot would have a marker for each customer located at the intersection on the grid where number of units meets number of claims. A visual representation of a relationship will show a pattern where the line of best fit (trend line) angles up or down. Qualitative data may be added to make the markers a different color for each value group as well.

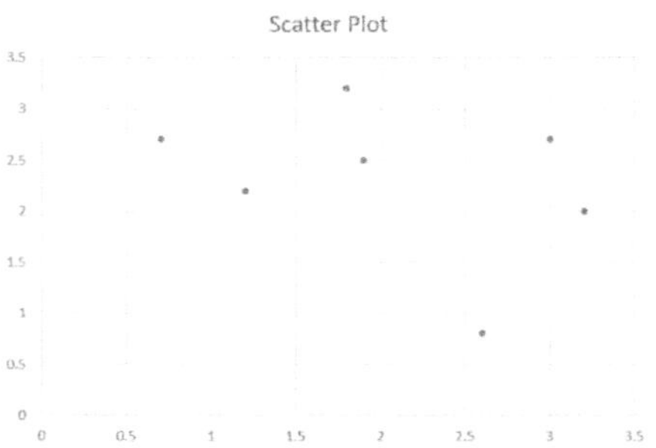

Bubble

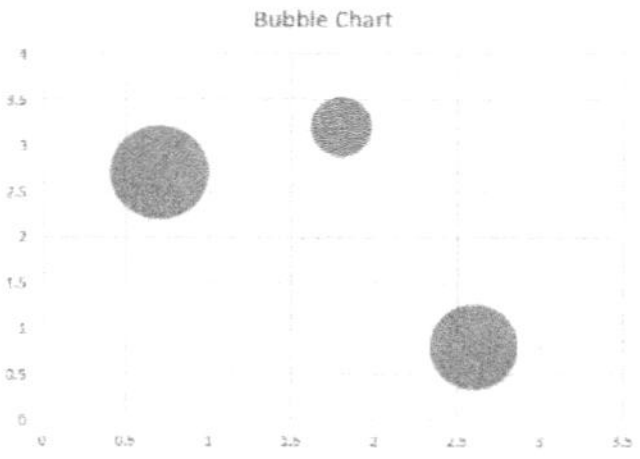

A bubble chart can display more than two variables by changing the size of the markers according to a third variable. The drawback to trying to read a bubble chart is that you often must visualize where the center of the bubble is located on the grid to determine value of the *x* and *y* variables. The bubble size is also less than helpful in determining a precise value for the third variable and comparing similar sizes of bubbles can be difficult. Another issue often encountered with a bubble chart is that the bubbles will overlap one another, further distorting the ability to identify precise values. For these reasons, scatter and bubble charts are typically used when the specific datapoint values are less important than the relationships between the markers. Clusters of markers indicate data that are similar across records. The patterns tell you more than the individual markers.

Box and Whisker

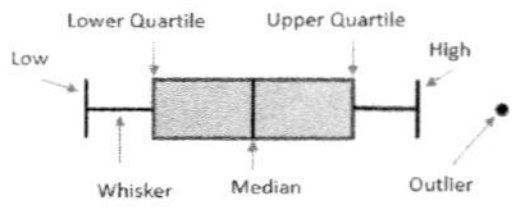

The box and whisker plot (or box plot) is a great way to understand a lot about the distribution of your data, but only if you can read one. I find that many people have seen them, but few really understand what they are looking at. Let's begin by looking at the different components that make up the box and whisker. The box and whisker can be oriented horizontally or vertically with the line at the far left or bottom represents the low number in the range of data. The line at the other end identifies the high number in the range. These lines are connected to the box by whiskers. The two ends of the box represent the lower and upper quartile and the line in the center is the median. Recall that the median is the middle number when the data is arranged in order. If you split your list into four equal parts, you get quartiles. So, the box and whisker plot is a picture of that list. The longer any one of the box halves or whiskers is an indication of a larger variance in the data. Consider the list of numbers 0,4,8,9,10,11,11,12,13. The median is 10. The lower quartile is 8 and 0 is the minimum. The upper quartile is 11 and the max is 13. This data in a box plot would look like this. Notice that the lower whisker is significantly longer than other parts of the box and whisker plot. This shows you that a quarter of your data is between 0 and 8 (a range of 8) and the ranges of the other three parts is only 1 or 2. If you see any individual data points plotted outside the range of the box and whiskers, those points represent outliers that were significantly different enough to not include in the range of the plot. When multiple box and whisker plats are displayed together, it becomes very easy to compare distributions of multiple subjects. This method offers much easier comparison that trying to compare multiple distribution histograms or density curves.

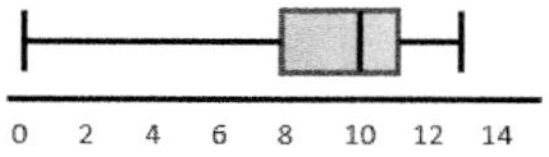

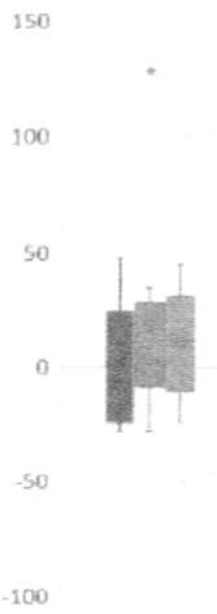

Treemap

A treemap visualization provides a visual comparison of measures of values by translating those values into rectangles grouped by category and sized according to the value being measured. This makes it easy to spot similarities and patterns and more easily displays all values in a single visual that a bubble chart for example where the marks can overlap and obscure one another. One criticism I have of this type of visualization is the amount of space it takes up. This is especially true if there are many sub-branches with many leaves and you want to be able to label everything. If the focus is only on identifying the data with the largest values, this may not be an issue.

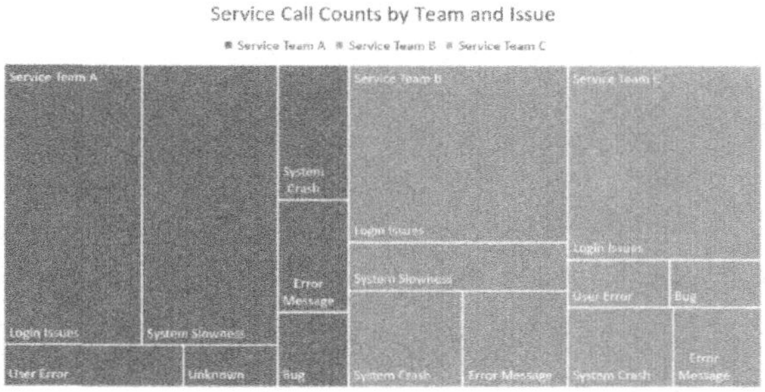

Sunburst Charts

Sunburst charts are radial treemaps. They are called ring charts as well. With the sunburst chart it is easier to see the difference between branches, stems, and leaves as the hierarchy is a little easier to see. It shows the hierarchy using concentric rings, each ring corresponding to a level in the hierarchy. The segments of the ring are sized according to the value associated with each category. Unfortunately, there seems to be a bit more difficult to include labels that are legible when there are many elements included in the chart. Like the treemap, if the focus is only on identifying the data with the largest values and the hierarchical nature of the data, the sunburst may be an effective visualization.

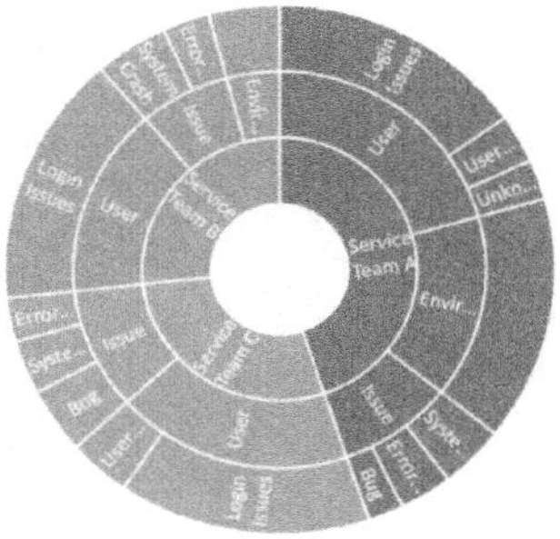

Heatmap table

A heatmap is a tabular visualization where each cell of the table is shaded according to the value in that cell. Typically, the higher the value, the darker the shading on the cell. Patterns are very easy to spot in a heatmap, and because of the consistent sizing of the cells (unlike treemaps and sunbursts) is it much easier to see the data details if included in the table. Heatmap visualizations will typically include a legend that identifies the values associated with each color if the color assignment is based on a fixed set of colors and ranges, or the legend will show the minimum and maximum of the range with a continuous color spectrum across the range of values.

	Mon	Tue	Wed	Thu	Fri	Sat	Sun
North	120	112	132	91	84	19	0
South	111	99	123	98	80	22	0
East	121	92	93	97	79	14	0
West	94	96	110	94	90	12	0

Geographic Heatmap

The heatmap concept can be applied to any graphic, but one that you will commonly encounter is the geographic heatmap. The focus of the map could be the world, specific continent, or country all the way down to the street level depending on the scope of the analysis you are viewing. Often these visualizations will allow you to navigate around the map and zoom in and other such interactivity. There are a couple different ways the heatmap may be filled. The heatmap may color in complete geographic objects such as country in the example, or it may look for like a weather radar map with intensity shown along a gradient at specific latitude and longitude coordinates.

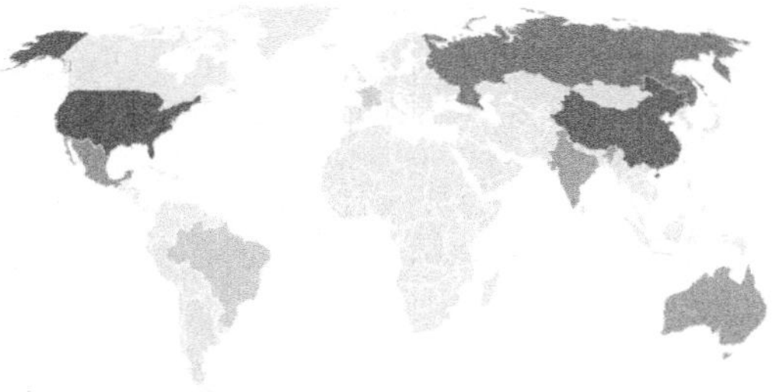

Funnel Chart

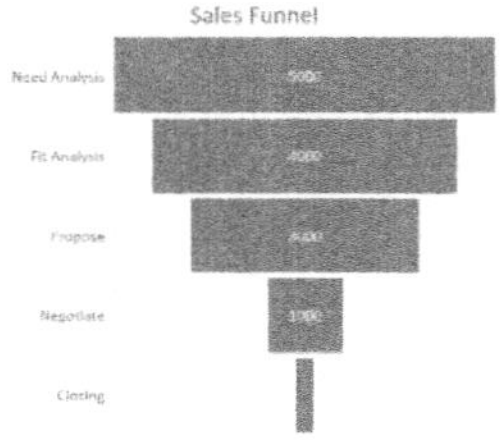

Funnel charts are very common among sales organizations where they are used to illustrate the sales revenue in the sales pipeline. Each of the sales stages are generally reflected in the chart with a rectangular or trapezoid-shaped area for each sales stage sized according to revenue. This typically results in a chart that is shaped like a funnel or inverted triangle. This type of chart is useful in understanding any issues in the sales process such as a very high dropout rate or a weakening pipeline indicated by the top portion of the funnel appearing smaller than the later stages in the process.

Pictograms

Pictograms are typically vertical or horizontal bar charts made up of small images rather than just a bar. This can make visualizations appear more interesting, but I would caution you to examine pictograms carefully, particularly pictograms you may see in the media. Pictograms are frequently used when the creator of the visual wants to distract you from the actual content of the measurements depicted. One of my favorite assignments in my statistics class in graduate school involved bringing to each class a chart from a newspaper with my own assessment of the flaws in the chart or study behind the data. They were almost always pictograms. Usually, the size of the images or number of images shown is meant to reflect the value, but often these charts lack any axis or properly proportioned scale.

Gauge Charts

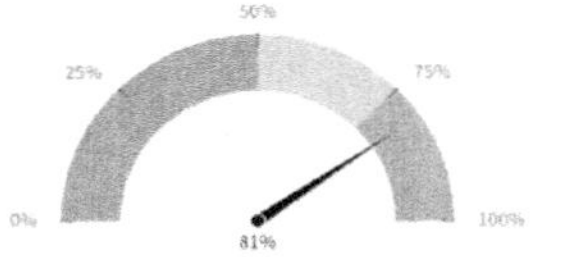

Gauge charts are graphical depictions of a metric value in the form of a gauge of some sort. It may look like a gauge you might see on a vehicle dashboard, or a thermometer that fills in as the value grows higher. There is no real limit to the visual design. The gauge chart will generally depict a single metric but could contain multiple by adding additional pointers to the gauge. There may also be some ranges included to indicate bad, or good ranges. Red, yellow, and green are often used as these stoplight colors have well-established meanings. Gauge charts add interest to visualizations but should be read carefully as there may be some interpretation required of the reader to fully understand the data displayed.

I have attempted to cover most of the most common charts that you are likely to encounter in the workplace. There are many other specialized charts and visualizations that, if well designed, you should be able to read and understand based on your knowledge of the above charts. Bear in mind that my descriptions of each of these chart types are just the beginning of what could be included in the chart. There are some indicators that provide additional information that may be included in most any of these charts.

You may find that some charts include reference lines. These reference lines can indicate trends in the data, a fixed value such as a target or goal, or the value of some descriptive measure such as average or median. Usually, any reference lines added to charts are labeled clearly so you know what they may be. Trend lines are usually shown as a line travelling through the center of the data and is calculated by identifying the statistical middle of the datapoints along the x axis. This is sometimes referred to as the line of best fit. You may at times see a trend line go from a solid line to a broken or dotted line. Typically, any lines that go from solid to broken are indicating estimated future values.

Another common strategy for adding additional information to charts is through color. Some charts use color to indicate intensity, like the heatmaps. Others use color to distinguish between groups or categories of data. There should be a legend that explains the meaning of the different colors used in a data visualization.

When reading data presented in charts, be sure to examine all elements in the chart. Legends, labels, captions, colors, sizes, orientations, and images all mean something or provide information about the data. If these things are missing or not explained, then the developer of the data visualization is not providing you the information you need to fully understand the data, thereby introducing bias to the analysis.

PRESENTING TO CONVEY MEANING

Sharing data with others is a task that everyone in the workplace finds themselves doing more frequently as the value of data increases in the business world. As a data literate individual, you will want to ensure that you are sharing data in a way that is easy to understand, is accurate and meaningful, and can be used to answer relevant business questions. The more you appreciate data and what data can do for you, the more you will find yourself becoming critical of data of your own and data shared from others. There is also a responsibility that you assume when you share data with others. This responsibility is integrity. Some of the things you will learn in this section of the book are meant to help you avoid inadvertently creating data visualizations that are misleading. I am trusting you to use this information only for good, and not to intentionally mislead others. The goal should always be to answer a business question, so that is where we will begin in this section. Then we will discuss selecting the right data and examining those data to work out the best way to answer the question. Finally, we will select the right visualization for the job. Earlier you learned a little about how to recognize and read data visualizations. The information in this section will help you select the right visualization according to the business question. Even if you are just using normal office applications rather that fancy reporting tools, it is always more effective to present the data in a meaningful way.

12
BEGIN WITH A QUESTION

The goal of collecting and examining data is making data-driven decisions. We want to be able to answer questions we encounter in the workplace with the confidence that good data gives us. Using data to answer the question rather than intuition or guessing or based on what is easier is more reliable and should lead you to better decisions. This, of course, is assuming you have formulated a good question, have appropriate data, and are able to understand those data well enough to formulate an answer. You cannot stop there. You should also be prepared to present your evidence. Show how the data lead you to the answer by sharing the data with others.

If your answers are only as good as your data, then perhaps your data is only as useful as your business questions. Business success has always been driven by great businesspeople making great decisions. Many of these businesspeople are finding that today's business is moving faster than their intuition can keep pace with. Businesses are turning to data more now than ever before, and this is a trend with no end in sight. Turning to data, companies are collecting more data more rapidly. Having all these data is a great advantage, but only if you start with a valid business question that leads to using your data in an actionable way.

There are essentially two approaches to becoming a data-driven decision-making organization. You can start by identifying the questions you need to answer to be successful and gather the data necessary to answer those questions. The other approach is to collect whatever data you can, examine the data, and find questions that you can answer in the data. I hope it is obvious to you that this second method is going to be less effective, but it also unfortunately the most common. Too many businesses realize that they have all this data and think maybe they should try to do something with it. The most successful companies start with the questions, collect the data they need, which may include data they already have, and examine the most appropriate data to answer the question. It is like the difference between using a GPS system to get somewhere or just wandering around town until you happen upon your destination.

To begin the transition to a data-driven organization, you should begin by identifying the things you want to solve according to your business's goals and objectives. Give some thought to the pain points and challenges that you face in your business. Chances are you already have some key performance indicators (KPIs) that you consider important to your business. You are probably already collecting data about these KPIs as well. A great place to start formulating business questions is around these KPIs. You might ask questions like:

- Which KPIs are strongly correlated to success?
- Are there KPIs that are not good indicators and should change?
- Are there additional indicators that should be considered key?
- How might we improve or refine KPIs to better drive success?

You may also have some strong performers in your company that you wish you could clone. Perhaps you have some business questions that you can craft that will help you understand how this exemplary employee does his or her job to be so successful.

- What does Mike do consistently, and can those actions be correlated to success?
- How does Mike complete his tasks?
- How does Mike's process compare to other strong performers and weak performers?
- Is Mike motivated in particular ways that are not typical?

Another area that is rich ground for formulating actionable business questions is your customer base. It stands to reason that a company that better understands their customer will better serve their customer and will be more successful. Work on identifying questions about your customers.

- What characteristics do our best customers have in common?
- What characteristics are more frequently seen in customers you have lost?
- Are there correlations between good customers and our interactions with those customers?

I could go on suggesting questions for you to ask, but it is more important that you be able to come up with some of your own, so I will share some tips for asking good business questions that you can use to craft some that are meaningful to your business. First, you want your questions to be relevant to your business and your level of the business you have influence over. If you are working in the mail room, you are not benefiting by trying to answer questions about sales incentive plans. Ask questions that will help you personally make the kind of business decisions that will help you do your job better, which will in turn, make the company more successful. If you are in the board room, you may have questions that are entirely different than others in the company.

Your questions need to be specific. Asking questions like "how do I increase sales performance?" are far too vague to be actionable. A more specific question about the business like "will changing the incentive plan increase sales performance?" will lead you to a decision about changing incentive plans. You can ask questions about what worked and what didn't work to determine if there are things that should be repeated or changed? "Which marketing events generated the most viable leads that led to sales?" would be one such question. You might even get more specific with "what was the return on investment of sponsoring the bowling team?"

Tying your questions to some measurable indicators will make determining and taking actions much easier. Ask about specific KPIs or other measurable variables so you will have a better idea of what action will likely change the performance. Also being specific about the timeframes or other parameters will help focus your question and the data necessary to answer those questions.

Specific questions that you can tie directly back to revenue-generating or cost-saving advantages are always good to ask. If your data can provide insights that make or save your company money, your data literacy will be rewarded. Just as good as making money and saving money is doing more and saving time. Ask questions about performance on the job and those who are performing well. You may just find some insights that will change the way the job is done, making it easier, faster, or more productive.

Once you become good at asking and answering the "what" and "which" and "how" questions about your business, you will find yourself wanting to ask some "why" questions. The other types of questions will help you understand what things are going well or not going well. The "why" questions will help you get to answers that enable you to truly understand your business and provide some visibility to the causes of success or failures. Knowing that your service team handled more calls last month than the same month last year is interesting, but it does not tell you any more than that. If you can determine why the service team handled more calls, then you have some insight that may lead you in several different directions. You may learn that they handled more calls because they received more calls due to a change in the product that negatively impacted usability. You may learn that they handled more calls because a recently implemented training program has made the service personnel more efficient. The possibilities are endless.

Another good source of business question are instances when you notice something in the data that seems out of the ordinary. Your business probably generates many descriptive analytics for tracking things that have happened. If you notice that the number of opportunities is up, but sales are down when there normally is a positive correlation between these two measures, you will want to ask some questions about why that is the case. You may not be able to perform a single analysis to uncover answers to the bigger questions like this. However, in asking the question and examining the data you will likely formulate several additional specific questions about the things you notice in the data.

Often the answer to one question leads to one or more new questions. As frustrating as that might sound, it is actually a great thing. This will lead you down a data mining expedition that will pay dividends in the amount of understanding of your business. You will find yourself forming additional hypotheses and questions that need to be answered to prove or disprove your hypotheses. You will find that a natural curiosity will serve you well as you work with data. The secrets held within are part of what excites me about working with data in this way.

13
SELECT YOUR DATA

Once you have a business question that you want to answer, it is time to select the right data to answer that question. You cannot assume that you already have the data that will answer the questions, so you should not automatically go to the data you have and start selecting from the dimensions and attributes you have at your fingertips. It is important that you do a bit of a needs assessment to determine which data will sufficiently answer your question. It is unfortunate that we do not always have access to all the data we would like to have. Attempting to answer a question with whatever data we have, rather than the data we need, we run a risk of not answering the question well enough to benefit our business. We must balance our desire for answers with the integrity required to answer questions completely and accurately.

The key to determining what data you need is starting with a detailed question and forming a detailed hypothesis. Suppose you are curious to know if prospects who attend a free webinar about your company's product are buying more frequently that prospects who do not attend the webinar. What data would answer this question for us? We will need data about the prospects – those who attended and those who did not attend the webinar including all prospects, even those who did not make a purchase. Using this data, we can identify sets within the data such as prospects who attended and prospects who purchased and those that did not attend and those that did not purchase. Every prospect should fall into two of these sets, so we will have prospects who attended and purchased, prospects who attended and did not purchase, prospects who did not attend and purchased, and prospects who neither attended nor purchased. We also need to think about the scope of the data. We do not want to include prospects who were never offered the webinar because the webinar did not exist. So, we will filter out prospects we pursued before the webinar was available. We also would not want to include prospects who have not made a purchasing decision since this would also cause bias in the data. Now we need to also decide if we want to work with the population or a sample of the data. Typically, in the workplace it is easier and always better to use the entire population. Since our population is well defined, it is not necessary to test a sample dataset and make inferences about the population. If you were wanting to perform an analysis about a large population like all people aged 18 and older, then we would not be able to examine the data for the population and would have to determine the best way to gather an unbiased sample of the population for testing. Since the scope of this book is the workplace, I will not dwell on this very complex problem.

Now that we have identified the data, we want to examine to answer our business question, we need to evaluate this data to make sure it will give us an unbiased answer. We need to know our data source. Are the data complete? Is it live or static data? Is the source trusted and is the data entered into the source consistent, free of gaps, and valid? We have already considered filters and timeframe, but we will want to consider if there are any events that occurred during that timeframe that may affect the results. There are many things to consider when selecting data for analysis. You will become very good at playing devil's advocate as you give your data critical examination for any possible biases. Keep track of any potential issues as you seek out any variables that could affect the results.

Speaking of variables, let's consider the different types of variables and how they may affect an analysis. We have already discussed independent and dependent variables. But there are several others we should be aware of as we dig into our data and make data-driven decisions. The independent variable is the characteristic that other variables cannot change. The dependent variable is reliant on other components. The fact that a prospect purchases does not change the fact that the prospect either attended or did not attend the webinar. The decision to purchase may have affected the purchase decision. Attending the webinar is the independent variable. Deciding to purchase is the dependent variable. The rest of the variables you need to watch out for and be aware of. They are not always avoidable, but you cannot simply ignore them either. The intervening or moderating variable is the theory that you are attempting to test. It represents the connection between the independent and dependent variable as a theorized association rather than an observation. In our sample, if you assume that prospects that were able to attend the webinar and purchase your product must have access to technology that some other prospects who were unable to attend may not have. That access to technology is an intervening variable.

Moderating variables can change the relationship between the independent and dependent variables by strengthening or weakening the effect of the intervening variable. If our prospects are from a range of industries, and one of those industries is independent restauranters, and the prospects from this industry typically does not invest in virtual meeting technologies, that may strengthen the intervening variable.

A Control variable is one that does not affect other variables because you are in control of those variables. This is most often present in a research study where you would have a control group that does not receive any change from the independent variables. You might think that using historical data would provide you the baseline that a control group would, but time must be considered.

Extraneous variables are always present in the workplace. Extraneous variables may affect the dependent variable but are not considered in our original hypothesis. Extraneous variables can change the results and change the way you interpret those results. In our example, there could be dozens of extraneous variables having a variety of effects. The video quality of the webinar, the instructor presenting, the economic status of the prospects, and so on. It is often the extraneous variables that lead to a deep analysis to better understand their effect.

Variables may be quantitative or qualitative. Quantitative variables are variables that involve numbers or amounts. These values may be discrete (countable) or continuous (unending) and should be considered and reported properly. Qualitative values are non-numeric. They may be binary (two values), nominal (no order) or ordinal (have an order). Our independent and dependent variables in our example are both qualitative and binary. Did the prospect attend the webinar, yes or no. Did the prospect purchase, yes or no. If we were trying to relate webinar attendance with purchase total, the analysis we perform would be different.

Confounding variables are those that can hide the effect of another variable. Confounding variables can introduce bias and invalidate your analysis. An extraneous variable becomes a confounding variable if it obscures the effect of the independent variable on the dependent variable in a significant way. If it turns out that only prospects who are in the north eastern part of the country are attending the webinar and purchasing your product, the location may be a confounding variable. Perhaps there is something about that geographic region that you have not considered that is affecting the purchase decision rather than the webinar. Often, confounding variables will lead you to adjusting your analysis to minimize their effect. This can be done by adjusting the parameters to account for the confounding variable. You may add additional sets that include or exclude data based on the additional variable or split your analysis and look for relationship between the confounding variable and dependent variable by making the confounding variable your independent variable. You may also consider restricting your data, especially if the confounding variable is only present for a particular section of your timeline. You might even combine your independent variable and confounding variable to create a new composite variable to examine.

Finally, composite variables are a combination of two or more variables that when combined make a more complex independent variable. Perhaps the combination of webinar attendance and some other touchpoint such as a marketing campaign is really what is affecting the purchase decision.

Regardless of what variables you identify and account for in your analysis, the data you select and the relationship between the independent and dependent variables will only allow you to infer some sort of cause and effect. It is very difficult and complex to prove causation in most cases. Often the best we can do in the workplace is to carefully evaluate and understand our data well enough to draw some conclusions, make some decisions, observe the changes, and evaluate again. Data literacy is an iterative development and awareness that will help you make not only data-driven decisions but will allow you to explain why you made that decision. The better we become at collecting and selecting data, the better the results of our analyses and decision making. At least that is my theory, and the observations I have made over my career have led me to the decision to write this book for you.

There is much more involved in becoming data literate than reading a book. Reading this book will only help you define what data literacy is. It takes practice and lot of curiosity to truly become data literate. I would posit that curiosity may be the most important trait of a data literate person. If you find yourself asking "why?" a lot, you have what it takes. That hypothesis, however, is subject to a lot of bias and confounding variables. If age is not considered, it would appear that most toddlers have what it takes.

14
ANALYZE YOUR DATA

In the previous section of this book I described a number of methods for examining data. In this chapter I will share some methodologies that will help you further analyze your data and some tips for recognizing certain issues so you can avoid them. To analyze your data to answer your business question and communicate that answer, you will start with the question, select the necessary data, then set out to understand that data well enough to formulate an answer to your question. This is where some of the math comes in to play, but don't let that scare you. I have often explained to students that I have tutored that you only need to know a few concepts to solve most complex algebra problems. All large problems can be broken down into a series of simple, easy-to-answer problems.

I will not pretend that some math skills will not make it easier for you to analyze data, but they are not necessarily required for data literacy. This book is about data literacy, not analytics, so I will try to keep the scope at an appropriate level. The topics I will cover will be guidelines for working with data in analyses and some concepts that are often misunderstood, even by people developing reports and dashboards.

Let's start with aggregation rules. Aggregation is the act of bringing data together into a cluster. You may have heard of apps or websites that refer to themselves as news aggregators. These bring together news stories from many sources together into one place. When we speak of aggregation as it relates to data, those clusters are things like totals and averages. Aggregations that you will want to be familiar with are count, distinct count, running count, sum, moving sum, running sum, average, moving average, running average, and median. There are several others that are less commonly used, but if you are at least familiar with these, you will have most aggregations you will encounter covered.

Counting is probably not a foreign concept to you, but for the sake of being thorough, I will start with counting. The count aggregations will typically result in an ordinal value that is a whole number (integer). Counting is often used to arrive at a numeric value for qualitative values. Count of employees or count of products or cases are common examples of workplace counts. Suppose you have a dataset of service cases and the assigned service representative is identified for each case. If you are wanting to know the case to employee ratio, you will need to get the list of service reps into a numeric value. Sounds simple enough, but if your table has a thousand records, and each of those cases has a service rep, that is one thousand service representatives. Count on its own is just a count of the rows in the table. What we want is a distinct count. The distinct count aggregation will only count each unique value once. Using the distinct count will give us a count of each unique service representative. The other count aggregation is the running count, which is the way we normally count beginning with 1 and adding 1 with each record. That one just seems obvious, but let's look at what each of these count aggregations look like in a table of data.

Case ID	Service Rep	Count	Distinct Count	Running Count
11111	Adam A.	1	1	1
22222	Bradley B.	1	1	2
33333	Carol C.	1	1	3
44444	Adam A.	1	1	4
55555	Bradley B.	1	1	5
66666	Carol C.	1	1	6
77777	Daniel D.	1	1	7
	TOTALS	**7**	**4**	**7**

Notice that the count and distinct counts appear to be the same when examining one row at a time. That is because the aggregation is happening on each individual row. The count of service reps on each row is one. The distinct count is also 1 because there is only one unique service rep per row. When you get to the total, the aggregation is now aggregating down the column across the rows. There are 7 rows of service reps. There are 4 distinct service reps in the table. The running count is also performing an aggregation per row in each row of the table, but in the running aggregation the value in the previous row is the starting point for each. So, as you move down the table, each row is showing the count of rows up to that point. These counts are not tied to the service rep name in the first column, so if you were to re-sort the table, the count values will not change. The count is based on the row of the table until it gets to the table aggregation, then it is based on all rows. You might think that this is like adding or the sum aggregation, and you would be right if every row of data has a value of one that you are totaling.

When you have a metric in your data that you want to aggregate, you will probably calculate a sum, average, or median. The most common aggregate is the sum, which is simply adding all the values together. There are a couple of special treatments of sum as well, but let's start with just a normal sum. Suppose our dataset includes the total call time in minutes for each service rep's case. The sum aggregate would be the mathematical total of call time in all rows down the table. The moving sum may total the last *n* values. In the table below, I am including a moving sum that totals the last three rows. The first two rows may not include any value, or depending on your data application, may include the total of up to *n* for the number of rows before reaching *n* records. A moving sum can be an interesting way to identify trends in the data as the numbers will increase or decrease based on the last several records. This particularly makes sense if your data is ordered chronologically. If a moving average is used, the number of values used for the calculation should be disclosed on the visualization, so it is clear what is be aggregated. The running sum is the total of values up to that point in the dataset. Plotting the running sum can help you see how consistent the values are, as a smoother line would indicate the running sum of very similar values, where a line that has a mix of sharp incline, mild inclines, and relatively flat sections would indicate more variety in the values being totaled.

Notice that the table below does not include a separate column for sum. The sum aggregate applies down the table, so the result is shown here under the Call Time column. The moving and running sums are dependent on the rows of the table, so their values apply to each row.

Case ID	Service Rep	Call Time (min)	Moving Sum (3)	Running Sum
11111	Adam A.	12.5		12.5
22222	Bradley B.	11.0		23.5
33333	Carol C.	9.8	33.3	33.3
44444	Adam A.	15.5	36.3	48.8
55555	Bradley B.	22.0	47.3	70.8
66666	Carol C.	4.5	42	75.3
77777	Daniel D.	18.0	44.5	93.3

	TOTALS	**93.30**		

If you were to total these moving sum and running sum columns, you could get a very inaccurate result. Most software packages will not do this automatically, but suppose you had this data in an Excel file and decided to drag that SUM calculation from the total cell across the other columns. Would you get a valid moving sum or running sum for the table? I tested this for you, and you can see in the results below that a very reasonable mistake of copying the formula from the totals cell and pasting it into the other two columns does not provide the totals we might expect.

	A	B	C	D	E
1	Case ID	Service Rep	Call Time (min)	Moving Sum (3)	Running Sum
2	11111	Adam A.	12.5		12.5
3	22222	Bradley B.	11		23.5
4	33333	Carol C.	9.8	33.3	33.3
5	44444	Adam A.	15.5	36.3	48.8
6	55555	Bradley B.	22	47.3	70.8
7	66666	Carol C.	4.5	42	75.3
8	77777	Daniel D.	18	44.5	93.3
9		**TOTALS**	**93.3**	**203.4**	**357.5**

Another aggregation that you will encounter often is the average. Average is not always the best metric for measuring central tendency as mentioned in an earlier chapter, but it is pervasive in most analysis you will encounter in the workplace. There are times when it is the right calculation to use, but even then, it is easy to use incorrectly. The average is calculated by dividing the sum of values by the number of values. In the table below, to get the average call time, we total of all the call times (93.3) and divide by the number of values that make up that total (7) to get the average (13.33) call time in minutes. If you have never thought about what an average really is, it might make sense to think of it this way. If the average call time of seven calls is 13.33 minutes, then the total time for seven calls will be 13.33 times 7 or 93.3 minutes. Average allows us to extrapolate a value when applied to a larger number of values. For instance, if I spend $5,000 to buy the five people on my team a new computer, the computers cost an average of $1,000 each. If I need to buy new computers for the rest of my company, I can get a good idea of the cost by multiplying the number of computers I need to buy by $1,000.

Case ID	Service Rep	Call Time (min)	Moving Avg (3)	Running Avg
11111	Adam A.	12.5		12.5
22222	Bradley B.	11.0		11.75
33333	Carol C.	9.8	11.1	11.1
44444	Adam A.	15.5	12.1	12.2
55555	Bradley B.	22.0	15.77	14.16
66666	Carol C.	4.5	14	12.55
77777	Daniel D.	18.0	14.83	13.33
	AVGS	**13.33**		

Moving and running averages are applying the aggregation to part of the data. In the case of the moving average, I again am using three records, and so the moving average is totaling the last three call times and dividing by three. The running average is totaling the call times of the record and all records before the current record and dividing by the number of rows so far. These moving and running metrics are useful in visualizing the trend of the data and can make the chart for a dataset with many records look a bit nicer as the moving average will form a smoother line than plotting all the call times.

Once again, you will notice that I have not included a final average for the moving and running average columns. Especially with averages, aggregating the aggregates is an easy mistake to make. If I were to calculate an overall average of these columns, I would get a value that does not reflect what most people will expect. This mistake is especially dangerous with averages because the error will not be nearly as obvious as a sum of sums. In the table below the overall average time is 13.33 minutes. The average of the moving averages is a very similar 13.56.

	A	B	C	D	E
1	Case ID	Service Rep	Call Time (min)	Moving Avg (3)	Running Avg
2	11111	Adam A.	12.5		12.50
3	22222	Bradley B.	11		11.75
4	33333	Carol C.	9.8	11.10	11.10
5	44444	Adam A.	15.5	12.10	12.20
6	55555	Bradley B.	22	15.77	14.16
7	66666	Carol C.	4.5	14.00	12.55
8	77777	Daniel D.	18	14.83	13.33
9		**AVGS**	**13.33**	**13.56**	**12.51**

Before we move away from average, I want to mention a couple of similar issues involving weighted average and a phenomenon called Simpson's Paradox. I don't know how many times I have encountered this because it is too many times to count. Let's start with weighted averages. Any time you see a calculation of averages for several groups, do not assume the overall average is the same as the average of those averages. Consider this example:

You manage five sales offices. You track some metrics on your offices, one of which is average number of monthly sales. You calculate the average sales per representative for each office. You are also interested in knowing what the overall representative average is for all your offices. As you see in the table below, some offices have 10 reps, and some have 5. The average sales per rep is calculated for each office (sales divided by rep). If you calculate the average of those averages, you will get an average of 11.6 sales per sales rep, but this is not accurate. Across all offices, you have 35 reps with a total of 385 sales, which is an actual average of 11 per sales rep. What happened to that other 0.6 sales? Because the number of sales reps is not the same for every office, the averages are weighted. If you were to equalize the number of sales reps by doubling the offices with 5 reps to 10 and double their sales figure, the average for each office remains the same, but now the overall average is 50 reps and a total of 580 sales then the overall average will equal 11.6, the same as the average of averages. So, if we are working on something like this in our workplace, we are not going to adjust the real numbers to equalize the number of reps across offices to artificially weight the averages. In the workplace we should calculate the simple average using the totals for both values and never use the average of the averages.

Sales Office	Reps	Sales	Per Rep Avg
Dallas	10	100	10
Austin	10	90	9
Houston	5	105	21
San Antonio	5	50	10
Amarillo	5	40	8

This effect is also explained by Simpson's paradox where a trend is seen when two datasets are evaluated separately, but the trend disappears when the data is combined. This was very prevalent in many explanations of vaccine effectiveness statistics. With the pandemic studies the groups were usually age ranges rather than offices. Reporting the efficacy of an intervention by age group may make the trend sound positive for instance, but when all age groups are combined, the trend goes away. As an example of this, consider two age groups of 18-50 years of age and 50+ years of age. The older age group is only 10,000 people large, and the younger age group is 100,000 people. If you were to evaluate the efficacy of the intervention and calculate the percentage of the people infected even after receiving the intervention, we are seeing 40% of the older group still get sick and 10% of the younger group. Averaged together, that is 25%, meaning the intervention works three out of four times. But if you report these groups together and say that out of 110,000 patients, only 14,000 became ill given the intervention. That is only 13% so it is working 87% of the time. That sounds much better. If you are in the older age group and were only given this statistic, you might make a different data-driven decision than if you saw the statistics for the older age group alone.

Sometimes a weighted average makes more sense and sometimes it does not. You must really understand your data to know which measurement you should use. The context of your business comes into that decision, which is why domain knowledge as well as data literacy is important when evaluating your data.

Moving on from average, let's look at the median. As we learned earlier, the median is often preferrable over average due to it being less subject to the effect of outliers in the data. If we return to our earlier service call time data, we know that the average is 13.33 minutes. If we were to reorder this data, and identify the middle value, which in this case is the fourth of the seven values, we can identify the median as 12.5. Not too far off from the average. The cool thing about median is that the larger the dataset the closer median will be to the average assuming outliers are not present. In this case our median is smaller than our average. Do you remember which way the data is skewed based on this circumstance? This is a positive skew because the average or mean is greater than the median. The range on the lower side of the median is only 5.5 minutes and the range on the other side is 7.5 minutes. Since we know both sides have the same number of values, the tail is longer on the positive end of the scale.

Case ID	Service Rep	Call Time (min)
66666	Carol C.	4.5
33333	Carol C.	9.8
22222	Bradley B.	11.0
11111	Adam A.	**12.5**
44444	Adam A.	15.5
77777	Daniel D.	18.0
55555	Bradley B.	22.0
	AVG	**13.33**

Let's talk about some other principles that can affect your data analysis and data-driven decisions. It is not just bad math that you need to look out for. It is very easy to confuse correlation and causation, and often it is an error of looking for data that supports a decision that has already been made or digging for positives that are not there. Other times just expecting too much from your results or focusing on the wrong results. If you are good at formulating your business question and identifying the exact data that will answer that question and have all the data and those data are clean and well organized, then these issues may not affect you. Unfortunately, you are not that good or that fortunate. No one is. There is always more to think about and more to consider, and I have never seen a business with pristine data. Let's stop fantasizing and focus on getting better. Perfection, like absolute unbiased truth, does not exist here on Earth.

Attempting to prove causation is a fool's errand in the business world. No matter how many times you hear this and agree with it, falling for the causation through correlation trick is just easy to do. It is natural. We are curious, and we want to know why, and we have trouble accepting that we may never know. In the business world, unless you work in a lab, we do not have the luxury of setting up a lot of test cases with control groups to get closer to proof of causation. We can try, but if customers and money are involved, it will take decades worth of data to get close to a proof. Advancements in machine learning are getting us a lot closer, though. More on that later.

We can show correlation in our business analysis. We can prove that when this thing happens over here, this other thing seems to happen over there most of the time. That proof, however, is not of causation. You should work on getting in the habit of considering any correlation to be a suggestion that there may be a cause hidden in there somewhere. It is a suggestion, not proof. Expecting too much from data will probably lead your company to collecting a lot more data, buying more fancy tools, and hiring some data scientists. These are all good things but may still not get you the result you are hoping for.

It is a folly to believe you can simply collect more data and use the new technology to turn your company into one that makes data-driven decisions and has a data culture. The key is not the data. The key is not even the data scientists. The key is data literacy and the ability to formulate and articulate the business questions that they need to answer and then act upon. Talented data scientists and analysts and good data will certainly help turn your company into a data-driven superpower that makes good business decisions based on those data, but without the right questions to answer, you are just cleaning up data.

It is also a mistake to get these things out of order. A data-driven decision is not a decision that you made and then showed why it was a good decision using data. That is answer-driven data analysis. You should not use data to support decisions that have already been made. The goal is to use the data to help you make the right decision. People tend to see what they want to see. Try this: think about the last time you purchased a car. After you made that purchase, did you suddenly start noticing how many other people are driving the same model car? Your new car was in the forefront of your mind, so when something like your car is mixed into the cacophony of the world around you, it pops out and you take notice.

If you have made a decision, and you are looking for support in the data, you will find it. Similarly, if you are in serious need of a win, or you are about to go into a meeting to present to the boss and want to look good, you are more likely to succumb to the temptation to seek out only positive messages in the data. If you look close enough you can find a positive trend in some of the worst results. You will begin to justify filtering out things and introducing bias to get the result you are looking for. It is human nature, and a habit that data nerds like me despise. There is only one most correct truth. It may not be an absolute truth, but the right truth is there, even if it is not the most positive or most comfortable truth. Lying to yourself and others about the data will not help you make valid data-driven decisions.

Don't expect the answers to always be clear. The real world is messy. The examples in this book and the case studies you may have done in school are not reflective of the reality of the complexity of the workplace. There may be dozens of variables affecting the outcome of your analysis that you did not even consider or know were there before you began analyzing the data. You are not going to get a perfect bell curve distribution of data or a dataset that is perfect and free of errors and gaps. You cannot make business decisions in real-life with the same confidence you had in school. You will not be given all the data you need to complete real-world assignments. You will have to work with the data you have and do the best you can.

Also, be sure you are not introducing bias in your data by focusing on the wrong period, or too short or too long a time period. If you are not needing to make real-time adjustments to keep systems up and running or call centers covered during a rush, you probably do not need to focus on real time, up-to-the-second data. If you are making decisions about marketing campaigns, you may not need data from the period after the campaign ended, and you probably should use static snapshots of data rather than live transactional data. If your data warehouse only creates a snapshot once a week, you cannot use that data to identify daily changes to the data. If your data is seasonal, a third quarter to fourth quarter comparison may be less appropriate than a fourth quarter last year to a fourth quarter this year comparison. Time is something that affects almost every analysis and should be considered carefully. You know your business. Use that domain knowledge to inform the questions and the analysis you are completing.

Since time affects a lot of analyses, it is important to consider multiple angles when analyzing data. Just focusing on totals and averages will not tell you much about rate of change, velocity of deals, patterns of data according to date and time, and things like seasonality. Totals are great, and interesting. Everyone wants to know what total sales were last month. Would they not find it interesting to know how quickly those deals closed or how many salespeople generated the total sales?

My final point for you in this chapter is a sincere request for you to attempt to truly understand the data you are being presented, especially if someone else did the math for you and produced the charts. You must be confident in those data to make valid data-driven decisions, and you cannot be confident with data you do not understand. Ask how the data were aggregated and what filters were used and what time periods are represented. Ensure that you have what you need to answer your business question. There is a time and place for mining data for trends and patterns, but for data-driven decisions we need to know the question we are meaning to answer rather than the answer we mean to support.

15
PRESENT YOUR DATA

There will be times that you are only reading and evaluating reports and dashboards that others have built, but there are also times when you need to express something using data yourself. It does not matter if it is a sketch on a napkin or a multimedia display, if you are not presenting data properly, your message will be lost on even the most data literate of people. People who are well-trained in presenting data still make mistakes when it comes to choosing the best way to illustrate and visualize data. Sometimes those well-trained individuals will purposely obscure data to present the message they want you to receive. Some of the things you will read about in this chapter can be used to properly or improperly present data, but I implore you to let the data speak for itself. Nothing good will come of improperly used data. It will either lead you astray or damage the trust others have in the data.

The most important thing you can do when presenting data to others is to select the best visualization for your data. You want to go back to the question you are answering with the data, and based on that question, identify the type of visualization that will best illustrate the answer. You will find that your question, if well-formed, will be asking one of four things. How do those data compare to those data? How are the data distributed (spread out over a range)? What relationships exist between those data and those data? What are the data composed of? Once you have identified to which of these four your question belongs, you then consider the variables or conditions you are investigating and select a chart that best fits the data.

One important note here is that you must select a chart that best fits the data, not select data that best fits the desired chart or select the chart that your boss asked for and cram your data into it. The chart selection is also a data-driven decision. While it may be true that executives tend to prefer simple pie charts and bar charts, if the question they have you answering requires a scatter chart, do not try to force it into any other chart type or you will distort the meaning and message of your data, and ultimately fail to answer the question.

Before we get into the specific chart selections, I want to argue against ever using a three-dimensional chart style. There are so few exceptions to this rule, that I am comfortable saying that you just shouldn't ever do it. Visually, 3D charts may look appealing and flashier than a flat two-dimensional chart, but by using the third dimension you are adding what I call visual bias. We are typically measuring data using an *x* and *y* axis. We may use a third variable to adjust the size of a bubble in a bubble chart for instance, but rarely are we plotting the third dimension on the *z* axis. By displaying a bar chart in 3D, the height of the bar is shown on the *y* axis, the category on the *x* axis, but the *z* axis is completely arbitrary and has no meaning. Visually it adds surface area that is not controlled by any measure and makes the bars look artificially larger than the measures they are meant to convey. A three-dimensional pie chart is even worse, as not all the wedges are artificially larger, only the ones on the side of the chart that shows the depth with that meaningless third dimension. There is only one chart type that I can think of that would call for rendering in 3D, and that is the 3D area chart. I have never needed this chart type in the thousands of reports I have developed for companies across hundreds of industries. I did not even include it in the visualizations discussed in chapter eleven. If you ever need to show the distribution of data using three variables, then the 3D area chart is a valid option and the only exception I am willing to make to the no 3D charts rule.

I will venture a guess that most of your business questions will involve some sort of comparison of data, either to other data or the same data over time. Time is such a common element in data so I will begin with comparing data over periods of time. Some considerations you want to have when visualizing a comparison of data over time are the number of time periods you want to show, the number of categories you want to describe, and is the data cyclical or not. If you are only charting a small number of periods, say 5 or less, then a column bar chart or line chart will be best. If you have more than a few categories, then you should consider the line chart. If you are needing to compare your data with other data for a few categories, you should use a column bar if there are not many items to display or a horizontal bar for a larger number of items. The horizontal bar is easier to read than a column bar when there are many items to display. If you have more than a few categories, a table is probably best. Another option would be something called small multiples, which is just a table with charts in the cells of the table rather than numbers or text. The decision table below can help by suggesting a valid chart type. Just read from left to right, selecting the appropriate section of the statement.

I need to compare data	across time	for 1-4 periods	for 1-3 categories:	Use a column chart
			for many categories:	Use a line chart
		for many periods	for cyclical data:	Use a radar chart
			for non-cyclical data:	Use a line chart
	to other data	for 1-4 categories	and just a few items:	Use a column chart
			and many items:	Use a horizontal bar
		for many categories:		Use a table or small multiples

Another common type of question we ask of our data is about what the data is made up of. This is usually looking at different parts of the whole or changes by category or over time. The charts that are most useful for displaying this type of data are those that show data split into multiple pieces like area charts, stacked bar charts, and pie charts. When we consider the composition of the data, we must consider things like the complexity of the composition or the number of components we need to evaluate. Many components make visualizations more difficult to read, so you may consider breaking the data down by additional categories and using multiple charts to get to the level of detail necessary to show all the data.

I need to dissect data	that is not moving	to show a share of the whole	for 1-5 categories:	Use a pie chart.
			for many categories:	Use an area chart.
		to show additions and subtractions to the whole:		Use a waterfall chart.
		to show the pieces of the pieces of the whole:		Use a radar chart.
	changing over time	for 1-4 periods	showing relative or absolute differences:	Use a stacked bar chart.
			showing only relative differences:	Use stacked filled bar.
		for many periods	showing relative or absolute differences:	Use stacked area chart.
			showing only relative differences:	Use stacked filled area.

Showing the distribution or density of data is commonly used for analyses involving statistics and grouping not by categories but by how many records are associated with each measurement. This may be an actual value associated with a record or the distance from a mean or median. This comes up most in industries where testing of products takes place or tracking of student performance or other lab testing scenarios are prevalent.

I need to show distribution of data	of a single variable	with not many data points:	Use a histogram bar chart.
		with many data points:	Use a density curve chart.
	of two variables:		Use a scatter chart.
	of three variables:		Use a 3D area chart.

Showing relationships between data is an activity that usually leads to some inferences about what makes the data change or how one variable typically looks based on the value of another variable or variables. There are only two common charts that are very good at visualizing relationships in data, the scatter plot, and the bubble chart. I often see line charts used when trying to show relationships, but this is because people often confuse relationships and comparisons. While you can infer some relationship on a line chart if two lines seem to move similarly or in opposite ways across the chart, the line chart of this type is really performing a comparison between two independent variables over time where a direct relationship is not necessary or assumed. The scatter plot is showing the relationship between independent and dependent variable where a relationship is hypothesized between the two variables.

I need to see the relationship between	two variables:	Use a scatter chart.
	three variables:	Use a bubble chart.

The chart suggestions I am making here are not necessarily the best chart for your data and I am not claiming that these are the only charts that can be used. There are other considerations, but these suggestions will get you started in the right direction. The table below contains all the charts I described in chapter 11 with a list of the types of analysis the charts are well suited for. The best chart for your specific data set is a decision that you will want to make based on how easy it would be for someone not familiar with the data to understand the message you are communicating with your data.

	Used to:			**Used to show:**					
Chart Type	Examine Data	Share Data	Watch data	Single Value	Categorical data	Time-based data	Components	Density	Relationships
Single Metric	•	•	•	•					
Table		•	•	•	•				
Pivot Table		•	•		•		•		
Pie Chart	•						•		
Donut Chart	•						•		
Area Chart	•	•	•			•			
Stacked Area	•	•	•			•	•		
Filled Area	•	•	•				•		
Column	•	•	•		•				
Grouped Column	•	•	•		•				
Stacked Column	•	•	•				•		
Histogram	•							•	
Density Curve	•							•	
Horizontal Bar	•	•	•		•				
Stacked Horizontal Bar	•	•	•				•		
Grouped Horizontal Bar	•	•	•		•				
Dot Plot	•	•						•	
Waterfall Chart	•	•	•				•		
Bullet Chart			•		•				
Line Chart	•	•	•			•			
Multi-Line Chart	•	•	•		•	•			
Dual Axis Chart	•	•	•		•	•			
Pareto Chart	•		•				•		

	Used to:			Used to show:					
Chart Type	Examine Data	Share Data	Watch data	Single Value	Categorical data	Time-based data	Components	Density	Relationships
Radar Chart	•		•		•				
Scatter Plot	•								•
Bubble Chart	•				•				•
Box and Whisker Plot	•							•	
Treemap	•	•	•				•		
Sunburst Chart	•	•			•		•		
Heatmap	•	•	•						•
Geographic Heatmap	•	•	•		•				•
Funnel Chart	•	•	•				•		•
Pictogram		•			•				
Gauge Chart		•	•	•	•				

I wish I could provide you with a comprehensive list of all the available charts and visuals that can be used to analyze, share, and monitor data. Doing so, however, would be giving you more options than you will ever be able to use, and the list would be incomplete soon after I put the last chart on the list because new chart types are being imagined all the time. You may even come up with something unique of your own. Most likely what you will dream up will be a variation of one of the charts in the above list.

Just like the different characteristics of business questions and characteristics of data, there are some characteristics of charts that can be identified. Lines on charts will generally show movement over a timeline or ordered process with the vertical height based on a value of the dependent variable. Bars typically show values by the length of the bar and show data across different categories or groupings. Any shape that is segmented into different sized pieces, be it wedges in a circle or rectangles split into smaller rectangles or areas filled to the top of a shape, generally show how much of a total each category fills. Shapes and colors are usually identifying categories or groupings.

The more you add to a chart, and often the more creative you get with different shapes and colors, the more risk of confusing those trying to read the chart and make sense of the data. I am certainly not advising against creativity and trying to add interest to visualizations, but there are some guidelines you should consider before you get too creative.

Let's begin with some things you should always strive to do when communicating data. Always review your charts for anything that distracts from the meaning. A lot of applications automatically add too much noise to charts by default. Extraneous gridlines, overlapping labels, and other elements that are not germane to the information you want to communicate. That brings us to the first guideline. Remove or de-emphasize any elements on the chart that are not the data. This includes gridlines, axis lines, legends, extra labels, and any graphic elements that do not have a purpose. The inverse is also true in that you should emphasize the data, especially any datapoint that is more relevant than others. Highlight chart components or add a label to just the critical datapoint so that the most important information jumps out at the reader right away.

Guideline number two is to reduce the amount of work the reader needs to do to understand the data. Rather than force others to follow gridlines back to the axis to understand the value of a bar, consider putting the actual values on or in the bars for them. If you want your audience to compare data, make it easy by placing the things to be compared next to one another. If the context of the data generally adheres to some order, show your data in that order. If you are tracking progress toward a goal or standard, indicate somehow on the chart what that goal is, and which groups have met that goal or not.

Guideline number three is to clearly communicate the purpose and content of the chart. You will want to include a title that references the relevant data in the chart or maybe even include the business question in the title. Use labels and annotations to point out important datapoints, but don't overdo it.

Now for some things you want to avoid doing as you design your visualizations. Your goal is to clearly communicate your results, so it makes sense that the first thing to avoid is misleading the reader. The values on the axis provide the scale of your analysis, so you are going to want to avoid cutting chunks of the axis out to save space. In most cases, you will always start your numeric axis at zero any time zero is a possibility. If it is a revenue scale, $0 is possible. If it is a time scale, you cannot go back to the beginning of time. In this case, your period for the analysis should have a start and end date. No matter the scale, you want the values along your axis to be evenly distributed. If you are using two vertical axis lines, these lines should be synchronized so that the height on the chart has the same meaning regardless of which metric the line describes.

The second thing to avoid is what my co-workers and I like to call too much lipstick on the pig. Of course, you want your visualizations to be beautiful, but you mustn't value the beauty over the accuracy or legibility of the chart. Don't use three-dimensional formats. Don't smooth out the bumps in the lines because those bumps are there for a reason. Consider your colors carefully, and don't use multiple colors unless they mean something. Shadows and other effects will deter from the data, even if it does look cool and flashy.

The last thing I want you to avoid is doing too much with one chart. Multiple simple charts are more effective than a single chart with too much data. I believe one to four series or categories is ideal. When you include much more than that your charts begin to be too busy to read. I have seen multi-line charts that look more like a plate of spaghetti than a usable data visualization. Too many labels and difficult to read labels are not useful either. Even if your chart looks okay with all the datapoints labeled, if you are building a chart that will be refreshed with new data, you may wind up with overlapping and obscured labels given an updated dataset.

Visualization design is a large discipline. There are many great books dedicated to the topic. If you will be designing visualizations of data, I highly recommend you do some additional reading on this topic. If you follow the advice in this chapter, you should be able to craft a very usable data visualization without much trouble.

MAKING DATA-DRIVEN DECISIONS

Here is where things begin to pay off. You have formulated your question, collected your data, and examined those data to get to this point where you will make data-driven decisions. There is more to making good data-driven decisions than just looking at the results of an analysis or two and choosing a path. It is a common mistake to collect lots of data, make a decision, and assume you have done the right thing, and all is well. The results of that decision will begin to flow in, and you will find that sometimes even data-driven decisions can be bad decisions. If you do not accept the data that is telling you there was a bad decision made, it will haunt you. The goal is not to never make a mistake, but to recognize your mistakes early and take corrective action right away before too much damage is done.

Data can seem magical, but it is not fool-proof, and neither are the decisions we make using those data. If we are skilled and let the data inform our logical processing of business challenges, we will make better decisions, but the work does not end with the decision. In fact, the work of data-driven decision making should begin before the decision is make, continue during the decision making, and not end until well after the decision has been made.

In this final section of the book, I will share some best practices for making data-driven decisions before, during, and after the decision. I have also included a bonus chapter on Artificial Intelligence and Machine Learning as tools to automate decision making and what they can and cannot do for a data-driven company.

16
USE DATA TO INFORM YOUR DECISIONS

As a data-literate person, you understand the value of data and how data will help you make better decisions. Up to this point, we have discussed the need to formulate a good business question. We have covered data quality and collecting good data. We have looked at analysis and visualization techniques. But all of that was leading up to this point where we figure out how to use data to make decisions.

Let's think about what it means to make a decision. We make thousands of decisions every day, and many of those decisions are as automatic and natural to us as breathing. The mental shortcuts we develop from making all these decisions allow us to make decisions quicker and with less focused thought. They become automatic the more we make those decisions. Perhaps this is where reflexes and habits come from. We would not want important business decisions to be made of reflexive decision making. Thought should be part of decision making in the workplace. We should identify the options, consider the variables, and then make a choice. We are problem solving rather than relying on chance. We want to make rational decisions and unbiased decisions.

Have you ever wondered why life's big decisions (get married, buy a house, have a child) seem to be easier to make than deciding what to have for dinner? I certainly have. I did not struggle for a minute when deciding to have children. Perhaps I should have. I have gone hungry many times because I was unable to reach a decision on what to eat for dinner. This feels a bit like a psychological ailment. There is some science behind how the mind works when making decisions, and I feel better knowing I am not the only one missing a meal due to indecisiveness.

I am not a neuroscientist, but I am a data scientist which is almost the same thing, right? Some actual neuroscientists have determined that the anterior cingulate cortex, orbitofrontal cortex, and ventromedial prefrontal cortex are all involved somehow. The brain reacts differently to different types of decisions. Maybe they can figure out why hard decisions seem easier to solve that the simple ones. We don't need to know how it works, really, but the brain behaves differently when presented different types of decisions. When we are told what to do, the brain behaves in a way that is different from when we are deciding for ourselves. The brain also reacts differently when we are confident in our decisions that when we are unsure.

Other things also affect our decision-making abilities and the decisions we make. We naturally will make different decisions when we are very happy versus angry. We make decisions based on belief systems and values that may differ if someone with different values is faced with the same decision. Charged emotions around topics like politics, religion, climate change, discrimination, human rights, etc. will change the way you form your opinions and make decisions.

Smart people can make dumb decisions, and dumb people can make smart decisions. Often the decision-making process has less to do with intelligence that you may think. Having all the information, knowing all the data, will certainly give you an advantage when making a decision, but the emotions and human behaviors cannot be discounted completely. When you have all the data, it is easy to become overconfident. You can easily jump to a solution before critically thinking about the variables and easily make a bad decision.

Critical thinking is an important skill, but it is just that, a skill. It is something that must be developed and practiced. It has nothing to do with intelligence. You do not need to be an expert on a topic to make decisions using information about that topic. Critical thinkers who are highly logical will usually make good decisions, but they too can run into some issues. I am often accused of over-thinking. I am the type of personality that finds himself planning every conversation of the day ahead while in the shower. I will "zone out" and seemingly be daydreaming when I am just analyzing data in my head. This can make decision making more difficult because the anxiety around making a mistake can be paralyzing.

When we discussed selecting data, I warned against selecting data that you do not need as it could introduce confounding variables and bias. There is another issue that you can run into when trying to determine which data to use. Data overload is when there is so much data that you simply cannot process it. You can easily miss important datapoints that would inform your decisions in the vastness of the amount of data available. This can lead to someone having all the data still making a bad decision.

The last phenomenon I will share that causes perfectly capable people with the necessary tools to make bad decisions. That is the diminishing attention span of humankind. We are losing our ability to focus. Information is at our fingertips in seconds from a simple search online. Entertaining videos that are just short enough to not bore us are just a swipe away on our smartphones. We can ask our digital assistants to do the thinking for us. This effect then leads to the "just one more" attitude that causes us to stare at our phones for hours watching just one more video. We lose time that we would otherwise be using to think about actual meaningful things, which leads to either a rushed decision due to no time or a lackadaisical attitude toward committing the necessary effort to make a good decision.

When faced with a decision, you are battling many things that can impair your ability to make a good decision, so using data properly to inform those decisions is a huge benefit to you. When faced with making a business decision, you should first evaluate your circumstances to determine the right approach. Ask yourself what information you already have access to that will help inform the decision. Determine if the decision you are making is one that has previously been made. Are you validating an earlier decision or making a competing decision? Do you even need to make this decision? Determine if you need additional data and how and where you will get those data. Will those additional data make any significant changes to the decision, or make it more accurate?

You also will want to evaluate the question to determine if additional decisions need to be made before you can answer this question. Are there additional questions that need to be answered? Don't over-think this. It is possible to break every question down to a set of the lowest binary level decisions, but that is hardly ever necessary. If you have domain or contextual knowledge, it is okay to consider that knowledge in making data-driven decisions if you can still explain how you arrive at a decision using the data in conjunction with what you know about your business. Do not re-invent or re-evaluate long-standing accepted truths about your business unnecessarily.

As you are making your data-driven decisions, ask yourself if we really need to make this decision. I am often amazed by the number of requests I receive for data and analyses that are never used for anything other than to satisfy a passing curiosity. If you are making decisions based on data analysis, hopefully you have concluded by now that there is a significant effort required to do it well. So, wasting time to collect and analyze data properly to answer a non-significant question keeps you from doing meaningful work. Given that there is a significant investment of time and data, will there be an expected return on that investment from answering this question? Does the cost of answering outweigh the cost of not answering? Is there a cost to getting the answer wrong? You also need to think about the time it will take and determine if you can arrive at an answer in time to make the intended impact. The answer to a question that is given too late to act on is not only a waste of time and resources, but it is frustrating.

One other thing you should consider as you are working on making a data-driven decision is how you will know if you got the right answer. What will the right answer look like? What effect can we look for to know that the decision was a good one. Inversely, what would the wrong answer look like, and what can be expected to happen when the answer is wrong.

It is finally time to draw some conclusions. The final step in making a data-driven decision is coming to that decision using the data. You have collected and analyzed data, and theoretically you discovered some things in that analysis. This does not always happen the way you hope, but don't worry, the data is only going to inform your decisions, not make them for you. The best place to begin is often with the knowledge you already have. You know your business and have tons of data in your head already to help inform your decisions. By combining domain knowledge with data analysis, you have interpretation.

Companies make many decisions and assumptions. Developing new products, breaking into new markets, and making assumptions about what customers want. This is not new, and many companies have made the right moves to be wildly successful with just their domain knowledge. With the addition of data analysis, you can begin to test pre-existing assumptions and refine your knowledge to make better decisions. This is a cyclical process, too. Your newly made data-driven decisions will likely generate additional questions more often than final answers.

17
VALIDATE, ADJUST, AND IMPROVE YOUR DECISIONS

Data-driven decisions will ultimately help you make better business decisions, but they will also generate more questions that will help you refine and evaluate those decisions. You will not only determine if your decisions were right, but you will also want to determine if there are more decisions that need to be made to make your decision better. You may also learn that there were some questions you should have asked before making the decision.

The title of this chapter is a bit of a misnomer. Truly validating a business decision is probably not even possible. Probably the best you can do is set some goals that you wish to achieve by making the decision to begin with. There are very few business decisions that will solely determine business outcomes. There are always many other variables involved, and it is quite possible that the decision was a good one, but because of other unforeseen changes or variables that were not considered as part of the original decision, things did not work out as planned. When we make a business decision, we do not have the ability to compare the effects of the decision with what the effects would have been of not making that decision. There is no test you can run to determine the benefit of the decision you made. The best we can hope for is relating the decision to the perceived outcomes given the decision and any additional variables that may affect that perception.

Depending on the scope of your question you may not know right away if your decision was a good decision, but what you will know is what data you will need to evaluate the answer. If you are making data-driven decisions, you have become familiar with the variables that affect the outcomes. You know which data to collect, and you will already have determined the best way to organize those data and analyze those data to verify your data-driven decision.

Most of what we learn is through trial and error and making bad decisions can many times be beneficial in the long term, provided you validate your decisions and evaluate improvements that can be made. What we are doing is training our personal decision-making model. The more we train our mental model, the better we become at making data-driven decisions.

Your decision-making capabilities will improve as you evaluate decisions by asking yourself some questions about your problem and decision. Did you ask the right question in the right way? Were your objectives well-defined? How are you measuring results? Did you use the best data to answer the question? Are there any risks or tradeoffs? Is anyone else involved in the decision, and were they included in making the decision? Is this a decision that needs to be made again, and what would make the outcome different? Were there pre-requisite decisions that should have been made that would have changed the outcome?

As you evaluate your decision, you will likely discover some things you would have done differently. Take note of these things and consider re-evaluating your data and analysis to see if your outcome is significantly affected. You may even determine that you should repeat the entire exercise before communicating your decision. I liken this to trying to build something or perform some home improvement. Very rarely does a project at home get completed after only one trip to the hardware store. In the case of business decisions, rather than realizing you have the wrong size screws, you may find you used the wrong data or left out a variable. It is always better to perform your analysis repeatedly than to provide an answer that you lack confidence in.

You may also consider soliciting feedback from others. It is possible to get yourself mired down in looking at the details of the data that you miss a valuable perspective. Feedback from others helping you make and evaluate decisions is certainly favorable to the feedback you could receive if a poor decision is made because you missed something or did not have important information.

18
ARTIFICIAL INTELLIGENCE AND MACHINE LEARNING

Artificial intelligence and machine learning are technologies that are relatively new compared to the statistical analyses and mathematical systems that many are accustomed to. They have quickly become buzzwords in a data-driven business culture. You have likely seen business applications with a "powered by AI" claim, but sadly, many of these claims are made using the loosest of definitions for artificial intelligence.

Artificial Intelligence is a technique for building computer systems that exhibit similar behaviors and decision-making as humans. Since there are no parameters here to what human behavior or decision-making include, or more importantly exclude, it is possible to make a claim that almost any system is powered by AI. Applications are designed to support human interactions, designed by humans, so naturally they will do things a human would do.

Artificial intelligence is the broader of the two terms as machine learning is a subset of artificial intelligence. Machine learning goes a bit deeper and solves problems and completes tasks according to a set of rules. This set of rules are the model that the machine learning uses to train itself based on data provided. Recall from the last chapter we are training ourselves to make better decisions. That is exactly the behavior that machine learning is mimicking using statistical algorithms. These algorithms calculate relationships and monitor changes in data or even test multiple scenarios to determine which variables are the most relevant in solving a problem. Machine learning models are re-trained regularly to take advantage of new data and can predict outcomes that require more math than any human wants to do on their own.

There is an even a subset of machine learning that attempts to more closely mimic human thought patterns through the development of layer upon layer of neural networks. It is not too far-fetched an idea that we will be able to come very close to creating computers that think and have personalities. Don't let that keep you up at night. You are data-literate so you will at least be able to communicate with them.

Before this book qualifies for the science fiction section, let's look at machine learning that currently exists. There are two primary types of machine learning that are becoming more prevalent among analytics teams: supervised machine learning, and unsupervised machine learning. Supervised machine learning takes data and problems we know about and does a lot of math for us according to some rules we provide. There are a couple of ways this is achieved. If working with a classification problem, data is assigned to categories. An example here might be given all this information about companies who bought our product, which of these other companies are most likely to be interested in our product? The more data we can provide the model to train itself, the more accurate the result will be.

Another form of supervised machine learning is regression analysis. With a regression analysis, we are not predicting categories like "unlikely to buy" or "likely to buy" but predicting values like percent likelihood that a prospect will become a customer. This type of analysis is used to predict revenues, stock prices, probabilities of success, threats of churn, and many other common business problems. A regression model still needs a massive amount of data to train itself with and uses many more attributes of those data than a human could feasibly handle with a pen and calculator.

Unsupervised machine learning uses data that is not labeled. We have not classified the data and the machine learning model will learn about our data though clustering or dimension reduction. Clustering unlabeled data groups similar data together based on shared characteristics. The algorithms will assign relationships, identify anomalous data, and create labels for data that were not previously known or understood.

Dimension reduction plots data across many different dimensions to understand the data and define characteristics. This type of analysis needs a lot of data but can be very effective with clean and complete data to identify relationships in sets of data that would otherwise go undetected.

There are many different models and not all models perform as well as others depending on the data. Often a best fit analysis will take place to determine which model provides the best results. In some cases, a combination of supervised and unsupervised machine learning will be most effective.

As a data-literate businessperson, unless you are part of a data science team, you will not likely need to know how to work with artificial intelligence and machine learning applications. The technology is becoming more accessible all the time, so it may not be that long before we are all "powered by AI."

APPENDIX A
GLOSSARY OF TERMS

algorithm A set of instructions to be followed in calculations and problem solving.

artificial intelligence The ability of a computer to perform tasks that are typically performed by humans because they require a higher-level of thought.

attention bias Bias introduced due to an individuals reaction to external stimuli that affect their ability to focus.

attribute A bit of information that determines the properties of a field in a database.

axis A fixed reference line along a dimension being measured. The horizontal axis (x) typically measures the variable thought to be the cause of changes to another variable measured with the vertical axis (y).

bias Prejudice for or against something, person, or group compared to another.

big data Large datasets used to revel patterns, trends, and relationships. Big data is often unstructured and contain massive quantities of information usually about individual's behavior and interactions.

binary Something with only two parts or two values. Binary code is made up of only 1s and 0s. Binary data may be true/false, yes/no, on/off etc. *See also Boolean.*

boolean A binary variable with only two possible states of "true" or "false" often used in logical operations.

categorical data A variable that can have a value that is from a limited set of possible values.

causation The act of causing an outcome or effect. Causation is the relationship between a cause and effect.

central tendency The tendency of data to have values that group around the center of the range of values. Measures of central tendency include the mean, median, and mode.

character large object (CLOB) A collection of character data stored in a field in a database table.

citizen data scientist An individual who works in a field other than analytics, statistics and mathematics yet performs some analytical tasks and model building for machine learning technology.

communication bias Introduction of bias due to poor communication of data. Poor communication or inaccurate communication or prejudiced communication may cause communication bias.

composite variable A variable made up of two or more strongly related variables.

confirmation bias Bias introduced due to the tendency of individuals to look for, analyze, and recall data in a way that supports a prior belief or desired outcome.

confounding variable A variable that affects both the dependent and independent variable, causing a spurious association, masking the true relationship between variables being studied.

continuous data A quantitative variable that may take on any value between any two real values. Measurements of size, volume, or time are examples of continuous data.

control variable A variable that remains constant and is unaffected by any other variables during a study or analysis.

correlation A statistical relationship between two variables. If two variable change at similar scale and rate, they are said to be highly correlated.

cross-reference table A table used to link two other tables together by containing two fields that reference the primary key of each of the other tables. Also called a junction table or intermediary table.

data dictionary A repository of information about data stored in a database. A data dictionary may contain information about the meaning, format, or use of data among other attributes of the data.

data discovery The collection and examination of data from a variety of sources. Discovery often provides some understanding of patterns and trends.

data mining Similar to data discovery but involves large datasets and methods such as machine learning, statistics, and multiple data systems.

data science A field that uses scientific methods, statistics, mathematics, processes, algorithms and systems to gain insight from structured and unstructured data, and assists with applying those insights gathered from the data to make data-driven business decisions.

data warehouse A system used for storing and reporting and analysis of data. Data warehouses are the central repository of data integrated from multiple systems.

database An organized collection of data stored and accessed via computer interface. Databases vary in size from very small single files to massive databases spread across multiple systems.

dependent variable A variable whose value is dependent on another variable. The dependent variable is often denoted by y.

descriptive statistic/analytics A summary that quantitatively describes or summarizes attributes of data.

diagnostic analytics Advance analysis of data that intends to answer "why" some effect occurred or was observed. Diagnostic analytics usually involve data mining, drilling down, and correlations.

dimension A framework that categorizes facts and measures to facilitate data analysis. Typical dimensions may include people, places, products, time, and location. Dimensions provide structure to unstructured or unordered data.

discrete data A count using only integers and as such allows for a limited set of possible values. Discrete data are finite, numeric, countable, and usually not negative.

drilldown Any operation or transformation of data that typically traverses relationships or multiple dimensions in order to learn more about those data.

duplication bias Bias introduced when multiple people or groups publish results of similar analyses with variance in the results due to methods or source data analyzed.

equation bias Bias introduced when improper or poorly selected equations are used in an analysis. Intentionally or unintentionally using bad math will lead to incorrect and biased results.

exclusion bias A type of sampling bias in which some groups of data are excluded from analyses.

exposure bias Bias introduced when study participants are pre-exposed to information or conditions that alter their response to data collection techniques.

extract, transform, and load (ETL) Procedure of copying data from one or more databases into a destination database or data warehouse. Data may be transformed during this copy so that the data is represented in a structure that is conducive to how those data will be used.

extraneous variable Any variable that you are not examining that may affect the dependent variable or other variables impacting your data analysis.

first normal form Data presented in its entirety in a single table with no relationships or lookups to data in another table is considered to be in first normal form. Columns in a first normal form (1NF) structure cannot contain more than one value. Where multiple values exist, these values will appear one per row.

foreign key One or more attributes in a table that references the primary key of another table. This links the two tables in a relationship.

Hawthorn effect Phenomenon where individuals modify an aspect of their behavior when they are aware that they are being observed or measured.

Health Insurance Portability and Accountability Act of 1996 (HIPAA) This federal statute enacted by the 104th US Congress requires that safeguards be implemented to protect the dissemination of information about any individual's medical history or treatment.

independent variable A variable whose value is not dependent on another variable. The independent variable is often denoted by x.

intermediary table A table used to link two other tables together by containing two fields that reference the primary key of each of the other tables. Also called a junction table or cross-reference table.

Internet of things (IOT) Physical objects that have software, sensors, processors, and other technology that allow them to be connected to the Internet for transmitting and receiving data.

interval level of measurement/interval scale A quantitative scale in which each qualitative value is assigned a numeric value along a scale. The values are equidistant from one another and have a specific order. A Liker scale is an example.

intervening variable a hypothetical variable used to explain relationships between other variables. They are not observed or measured as they are hypothetical. Also called a mediator variable.

junction table A table used to link two other tables together by containing two fields that reference the primary key of each of the other tables. Also called an intermediary table or cross-reference table.

kernel smoothing A statistical technique that uses weighted averages of observed data to fill in the gaps between datapoints. This smooths out the line on a line chart.

key performance indicator (KPI) A performance measurement that is critical to the business used to evaluate the success of an individual's or organization's performance.

leading indicators Typically in reference to financial data, a leading indicator is some sort of event that statistically suggests that some related event will happen in the near future.

Likert scale A five or seven (never six) point scale commonly used on surveys. This scale is generally used to measure attitude or feelings about the subject of a question.

location bias A bias toward a particular location or area, either physical or online.

machine learning The study of computer algorithms that improve through repeated use of the data.

mapping table A data table used for mapping input data to a set of output data fields.

mean The mathematical average derived by totaling all values and dividing that total by the number of values in the set.

measurement biases Bias resulting from using incorrect data or inappropriate measurement methods.

median A measure of central tendency that is equal to the exact middle of the dataset when all values are listed in numerical order.

mediator variable A hypothetical variable used to explain relationships between other variables. They are not observed or measured as they are hypothetical. Also called a intervening variable.

moderating variable A variable that is used to explain the strength of a relationship between other variables.

natural language processing A field that combines linguistics, computer science, and artificial intelligence that uses language recognition to perform data analysis.

negative correlation A relationship between two variables that move (increase or decrease) opposite of one another. When one variable increases, the other decreases.

neural networks A computer system using algorithms modeled on the human and nervous system.

nominal scale A scale that uses tags or labels to identify values and categories to which those values belong.

non-relational databases A non-relational (or NoSQL) database stores and retrieves data that is modeled in a format other than the tabular relationships used in relational databases.

normalization The process of structuring a database according to a set of normal forms to reduce redundancy and increase integrity.

normalized (bell) curve A line graph shaped like a bell due to the natural tendency of data to normalize clustered around the mean.

No-SQL database A non-relational database stores and retrieves data that is modeled in a format other than the tabular relationships used in relational databases.

numeric data Data in the form of numbers rather than any particular language.

ordinal Categorical data type where the variable have natural ordered categories where the distance between values is not known.

outlier A datapoint that is significantly different from other datapoints in a set. Outliers cause a variability in the data analysis that may not be valid due to an anomaly causing the outlier. Outliers are often excluded from analyses for this reason.

overfitting Performing an analysis that correlates too closely to a specific subset of the data making it less applicable to the larger dataset.

pareidolia The tendency to perceive a pattern or meaning where there is none.

personal identifiers (PID) A subset of personally identifiable information datapoints that identify a unique individual. Criminals use PID to assume the identify of others.

personally identifiable information (PII) Any information related to an identifiable person. Improperly used PII in data eliminates anonymity and may introduce bias.

positive correlation A relationship between two variables that move (increase or decrease) together. When one variable increases, so does the other.

predictive analytics Analytics using a variety of statistical and machine learning techniques to analyze current and historical data to make predictions about future events.

prescriptive analytics Analytics using descriptive and predictive analyses to help businesses make better decisions or determine next best actions.

primary key One or more attributes in a table that uniquely identify a single record in a table.

psychometrics A field within psychology and education devoted to testing, measurement, assessment, and analysis of testing instruments and test results.

qualitative data Data that describe the attributes or classifications of an object. Classifications may be assigned a numeric value for analysis, but those numbers have no significance and only represent the classification.

quantitative data Data in the form of numbers or counts that describe the value of an object.

quartile A form order statistic that divides a sorted set of values into four equal parts (equal in count of datapoints).

ratio level of measurement/ratio scale The highest of the four scales, the ratio level values can be categorized, ordered, have equal intervals, and can be zero.

relational databases A database structured to use relationships between items stored in tables to connect data. Relational databases are usually queried using SQL.

reporting bias Bias introduced by selective reporting or withholding of information in an analysis. Can also be used to describe the tendency of people to under-report information available when responding to surveys.

sampling bias Bias introduced when a sample of the population is selected in such a way that portions of the population are more or less probable for inclusion that others. The sample does not accurately represent the population.

second normal form (2NF) In a relational database, the tables are related using keys to avoid redundancy. A relation in 2NF will have no partial dependency.

self-selection bias Bias introduced when participants are able to choose whether or not to participate. This is similar to sampling bias as the sample will include only participants who are more likely to participate in the study, which likely does not represent the population.

Simpson's Paradox A phenomenon in statistics where a trend may appear in groups of data but disappears or reverses when the groups are combined. Averaging of averages is a form of this phenomenon as the groups being averaged initially may be of different sizes, so when the averages of those averages is taken, it does not accurately represent the true average of the combined groups.

simulation Imitation of an operation of a process or system using a model that represents the key characteristics and behaviors of the process or system being simulated.

skewness A distortion or asymmetry from the normal bell curve distribution of data. The measure of skewness can be positive, zero, negative or undefined.

standard deviation The measure of the amount of variation of a set of values. A low standard deviation indicates that the values are less dispersed from the mean while a high standard deviation shows a wide spread of data over a larger range.

string data Data made up of a sequence of characters. Characters may be alpha or numeric or a mixture of both, but have no mathematical value beyond the character count that makes up the string.

structured data Data that complies with a pre-defined data model, making the data easily accessible and more convenient for analysis.

structured query language (SQL) Computer language used to manage, manipulate, and access data in a relational database.

time interval bias Bias introduced by a type of sampling error in which observations are made from only a specific time period therefore not representing the entire timeline.

trailing indicators Events that seemingly always occur after certain events or behaviors are observed that can be used as evidence suggesting those events or behaviors occurred.

underfitting Occurs when a data model is unable to identify the relationship between two variables accurately, generating a high error rate in the analysis.

unstructured data Information that does not have a defined data model or is not organized in any particular way.

variance A measure of dispersion indicating how far a dataset is spread out in relation to its mean.

verification bias Bias that occurs when repeated tests or analysis of the same data do not return similar results.

visual bias Bias introduced when the scale or visual effects of a data visualization lead the consumer of the data to incorrect conclusions based on the visual representation. Three dimensional pie charts are a good example of a cause of visual bias.

weighted average An average created from the multiplication of each component by a factor according to its importance.

APPENDIX B
ABECEDARIAN LUCUBRATION

The poem below is included in this book to serve two purposes. First, it is a literary example of what someone who is extra-literate might enjoy. Data literacy does not mean you know everything there is to know about data. You are able to read this book because you are literate in English, but you do not need to know every word in the English language to be considered literate. The other purpose is simply to satisfy my personal dream of seeing this poem published. I tried in 1992, but the world was not ready.

Abecedarian Lucubration

Afflatus Balladromic.
Catachresis Deblaterated.
Egregiously Fustian.
Grandiloquism Horrisonant.

Idioglossia Jabbered.
Kedogenous Logorrhea.
Macrology Nefandous.
Obviously Parisology.

Quisquous Risorgimento.
Sesquipedalian Textually.
Utterance Vecordious.
Word-painting Xenium;
Yielding Zeugma.

Michael Lairson – 1992

To the right I have included a short definition of each of the words in this poem, in case you are interested. The poem simply describes itself.

Abecedarian Lucubration: a solemn literary work that is the product of laborious cogitation arranged in alphabetical order
Afflatus: a strong creative impulse; divine inspiration
Balladromic: maintaining course towards a target
Catachresis: strained or paradoxical use of words
Deblaterated: babbled, prated
Egregiously: conspicuously and outrageously bad or reprehensible
Fustian: pompous or pretentious talk or writing
Grandiloquism: speech that is lofty in style
Horrisonant: sounding dreadfully; uttering a terrible sound
Idioglossia: secret speech or language; psychological condition in which speech is so distorted as to be unintelligible
Jabbered: rapid and indistinct speech
Kedogenous: produced by worry
Logorrhea: pathologically excessive (and often incoherent) talking
Macrology: Long and tedious talk without much substance; superfluity of words
Nefandous: Unfit to speak of; unmentionable; impious; execrable
Obviously: Ironically the only "obvious" word in the poem
Parisology: the use of ambiguous words
Quisquous: perplexing
Risorgimento: rising again; a time of Renaissance
Sesquipedalian: to the overuse of long words
Textually: or relating to or based on a text
Utterance: the use of uttered sounds for auditory communication
Vecordious: senseless, insane, mad
Word-painting: a graphic or vivid verbal description
Xenium: A present given to a guest or stranger
Yielding: producing a certain amount
Zeugma: literary device of using word to modify two other words with only one of which it is correctly used

APPENDIX C
MYSQL DATA TYPES

String Data

DATA TYPE	SPECIFICATION
CHAR(size)	0 to 255 characters.
VARCHAR(size)	0 to 255 characters.
BINARY(size)	Equal to CHAR(). Stores one binary byte.
TINYTEXT	0 to 255 characters
TINYBLOB	Binary Large Object up to 255 bytes
TEXT(size)	0 to 65,535 characters
BLOB(size)	Binary Large Object 0 to 65,535 bytes
MEDIUMTEXT	0 to 16,777,215 characters
MEDIUMBLOB	Binary Large Object 0 to 16,777,215 bytes
LONGTEXT	0 to 4,294,967,295 characters
LONGBLOB	Binary Large Object 0 to 4,294,967,295 bytes
ENUM(val1, val2, ...)	One value from preset options. Up to 65.535 values
SET(val1, val2, ...)	Selection of one or more preset options up to 64

Numeric Data

DATA TYPE	SPECIFICATION
BIT(size)	Bit value type (1 to 64 bits)
TINYINT(size)	Integer (-128 to 127)
SMALLINT(size)	Integer (-32,768 to 32,767)
MEDIUMINT(size)	Integer (-8,388,608 to 8,388,607)
INT(size)	Integer (-2,147,483,648 to 2,147,483,647)
INTEGER(size)	Same as INT(size)
BIGINT(size)	Integer (-9.223.372.036.854.775.808 to 9.223.372.036.854.775.807)
FLOAT(size, d)	Decimal (precise to 23 digits) Total digits in size and number of decimal places in d
DOUBLE(size, d)	Decimal (24 to 53 digits)
DECIMAL(size, d)	Fixed point number. Total digits in size up to 64. Digits after the decimal in d up to 30.
DEC(size, d)	Same as DECIMAL
BOOL	0 = false, 1 = true
BOOLEAN	Same as BOOL 1 or 0 (Also same as TINYINT(1)

Date and Time Data

DATA TYPE	SPECIFICATION
DATE	YYYY-MM-DD (1000-01-01 to 9999-12-31)
DATETIME	YYYY-MM-DD HH:MM:SS (1000-01-01 00:00:00 to 9999-12-31 23:59:59)
TIMESTAMP	YYYYMMDDHHMMSS stored as the number of seconds since the Unix epoch (1970-01-01 00:00:00 UTC)
TIME	HH:MM:SS (-838:59:59 to 838:59:59)
YEAR	YYYY (1901 to 2155, and 0000)

APPENDIX D
SQL DATABASE DATA TYPES

String Data

DATA TYPE	SPECIFICATION
char(n)	Fixed width up to 8,000 characters
varchar(n)	Variable width up to 8,000 characters
varchar(max)	Variable width up to 1,073,741,824 characters
text	Variable width up to 2GB of text data
nchar	Fixed Unicode string up to 4,000 characters
nvarchar	Variable width Unicode string up to 4,000 characters
nvarchar(max)	Variable width Unicode string up to 536,870,912 characters
ntext	Variable width Unicode string up to 2GB of text data
binary(n)	Fixed width binary string up to 8,000 bytes
varbinary	Variable width binary string up to 8,000 bytes
varbinary(max)	Variable width binary string up to 2GB
image	Variable width binary string up to 2GB

Numeric Data

DATA TYPE	SPECIFICATION
bit	Integer. Valid values are 0, 1, or NULL
tinyint	Integer (0 to 255)
smallint	Integer (-32,768 to 32,767)
int	Integer (-2,147,483,648 to 2,147,383,647)
bigint	Integer (-9,233,372,036,854,775,808 to 9,233,372,036,854,775,807)
decimal(p,s)	Fixed precision number where p is maximum total digits (1 to 38) and s is the number of digits after the decimal (0 to 38).
number(p, s)	Fixed precision number where p is maximum total digits (1 to 38) and s is the number of digits after the decimal (0 to 38).
smallmoney	Monetary number (-214,748.3648 to 214,748.3647)
money	Monetary number (-922,337,203,685.5808 to 922,337,203,685.5807)
real	Floating precision number

Date and Time Data

DATA TYPE	SPECIFICATION
datetime	From 1753-01-01 to 9999-12-31 with timestamp accuracy to 3.33 ms
datetime2	From 0001-01-01 to 9999-12-31 with timestamp accuracy to 100 ns
smalldatetime	From 1900-01-01 to 2076-06-06 with timestamp accuracy to 1 min
date	From 0001-01-01 to 9999-12-31 date only
time	Time only accurate to 100 nanoseconds
datetimeoffset	Same as datetime2 with a time zone offset
timestamp	Unique number that is updates every time a row is created or modified

APPENDIX E
ORACLE/PSQL DATA TYPES

String Data

DATA TYPE	SPECIFICATION
char(n)	Fixed width up to 2,000 charaters
nchar(n)	Variable width up to 2,000 characters
nvarchar2(n)	Variable width up to 4,000 characters
varchar2(n)	Variable width up to 4,000 characters
raw	Variable width binary string up to 2,000 bytes
long	Variable width binary string up to 2GB
long raw	Variable width binary string up to 2GB
blob	Large binary objects up to 3.99GB
clob	Single-byte and multi-byte character data up to 3.99GB
nclob	Unicode data up to 3.99GB

Numeric Data

DATA TYPE	SPECIFICATION
number(p, s)	Fixed precision number where p is maximum total digits (1 to 38) and s is the number of digits after the decimal (-84 to 127).
numeric(p, s)	Fixed precision number where p is maximum total digits (1 to 38) and s is the number of digits after the decimal (-84 to 127).
float	Floating precision number up to precision of 126
real	Floating precision number up to precision of 63
double precision	Floating precision number up to precision of 126
integer	Integer (0 to 255)
smallint	Integer (-32,768 to 32,767)
int	Integer (-2,147,483,648 to 2,147,383,647)

Date and Time Data

DATA TYPE	SPECIFICATION
date	From Jan 1 4712 BC to Dec 31 9999 AD
timestamp(n)	Fractional seconds precision up to 9
timestamp(n) with time zone	Fractional seconds precision up to 9. Includes time zone displacement
timestamp(n) with local time zone	Fractional seconds precision up to 9. Uses session local time zone
interval year(n) to month	Time period stored in years and months
Interval day(n) to second(n)	Time period stored in days, hours, minutes, and seconds

APPENDIX F
MS ACCESS DATA TYPES

DATA TYPE	SPECIFICATION
Text	Text and numbers up to 255 characters
Memo	Text and numbers up to 65,536 characters
Byte	Integer (0 to 255)
Integer	Integer (-32,768 to 32,767)
Long	Integer (-2,147,483,648 to 2,1417,383,647)
Single	Single precision floating point
Double	Double precision floating point
Currency	Monetary value up to 15 digits left of decimal and 4 to right
AutoNumber	Automatically numbers rows usually beginning at 1
Date/Time	Dates and Times
Yes/No	Can be yes/no, true/false, or on/off. Null values are not allowed
Ole Object	Binary Large Objects (pictures, audio, video)
Hyperlink	Link to other files or Web pages
Lookup Wizard	Allows selection from a list of values